* Where there
the enem... .... cannot
hurt you.
Roy Christian. — African Proverb.

THE ENEMY
WITHIN

THE ENEMY WITHIN

Encountering and Conquering the Dark Side

MARK L. PROPHET • ELIZABETH CLARE PROPHET

THE SUMMIT LIGHTHOUSE LIBRARY®

THE ENEMY WITHIN
ENCOUNTERING AND CONQUERING THE DARK SIDE
by Mark L. Prophet and Elizabeth Clare Prophet
Copyright © 2004 by Summit University Press
All rights reserved

Summit University Press
PO Box 5000
Gardiner, MT 59030-5000, USA
Tel: 1-800-245-5445 or 406-848-9500
Web site: www.summituniversitypress.com
Email: info@summituniversitypress.com

Library of Congress Control Number: 2004107853
ISBN: 0-922729-99-9

THE SUMMIT LIGHTHOUSE LIBRARY®

The Summit Lighthouse Library is an imprint of Summit University Press.

SUMMIT UNIVERSITY PRESS®

The Summit Lighthouse, *Pearls of Wisdom,* Science of the Spoken Word, Keepers of the Flame, and Summit University are trademarks registered in the U.S. Patent and Trademark Office and in other countries. All rights to their use are reserved.

Printed in the United States of America

08 07 06 05 04   6 5 4 3 2

CONTENTS

Recognizing the Enemy

The enemy within, the anti-self, the unreal self, the lesser self—there are many names for the part of us that sometimes sabotages our highest dreams and ideals. The early Christian Gnostics called it the counterfeiting spirit. It has also been called the dweller-on-the-threshold.

Everybody has one, but few are aware of its existence. Yet if we are observant, we will admit that from time to time we have all seen or felt the lesser self when it acts in ourselves or in others.

When we say the unkind words we wish we could take back, when we do those things that we know we should not do, when we neglect to extend love to friends and family, when our thoughts and deeds betray our highest wishes and aspirations, then we can know that we have had an encounter with the enemy within. But even if we recognize the encounter, few are prepared to deal with this enemy—or even know how to begin.

If you wish to overcome this enemy within, the first step is to recognize the not-self and understand how it works, which is precisely the purpose of this book. (In fact, your own enemy within would rather that you not pick up this book at all.)

You will learn that this enemy is often very subtle: the last thing that it wants is for you to know that it exists. For once you do, you are more likely to see through its ploys and traps. It most often prefers to live below the surface of awareness—like some phantom of the opera, hiding in the shadows and causing havoc in your life. This secretive nature of the enemy is one reason why it is called the dweller-on-the-threshold: it is a presence that dwells at the threshold of conscious awareness, where the conscious and subconscious minds meet.

Many of the saints of East and West have left a record of their own struggles with the dweller-on-the-threshold. Indeed everyone who has ever returned to God in the ritual of the ascension has had to wrestle with this enemy prior to their victory.

The apostle Paul confronted the adversary and wrote of his struggle between light and darkness in his epistle to the Romans: "For the good that I would, I do not: but the evil which I would not, that I do.... When I would do good, evil is present with me."[1]

Paul had his own name for the enemy within. He called it the carnal mind: "The carnal mind is enmity against God: for it is not subject to the law of God, neither indeed can be."[2] And so we see the dweller also appearing in the human ego, the human will and the human intellect when these are not tethered to our inner Reality.

We can think of the dweller as the animal nature of man, the part of us that has no light, but only a forcefield of darkness at its core. The dweller is a tyrant. Archetypically, it is often shown as a dragon or a beast. But it can be dealt with—and must be dealt with, if we are to find true freedom.

For most of us, daily encounters with the dweller occur in seemingly unimportant incidents. We live lives that are a mixture of the good (but not *too* good) and the bad (but not *too* bad). The dweller may emerge occasionally, but we think we have things "under control." We can continue in this way for many years, or even lifetimes.

But one day the confrontation will come, for the dragon ultimately wants all of us: it will one day emerge seeking to devour the very soul itself. The story of Saint George and the dragon symbolizes the work that the soul must accomplish when faced with this challenge. Through the power of the Christ, the dragon must be slain: we will have to fight the good fight and win.

The confrontation with the not-self is one of the most serious initiations on the path of the one who would be a disciple. It is indeed a battle of Light and Darkness. Each day, the dweller lurks at the threshold, seeking to gain entrance. It would enter to become the master of the house. But it is the Christ, and only the Christ, whose knock we must answer. So what can we do?

There is a path to follow and a road map that can lead us to the goal. It will take effort and striving, but we can overcome. In these lectures, you will find the keys that can help you in those day-to-day choices—and in the ultimate confrontation.

One of those keys is the spiritual community. Thus there have been many religious communities and mystery schools throughout the ages where those who desired to walk a spiritual path could find strength in joining with others with like aspirations. The first mystery school was known as the Garden of Eden—a place where many twin flames (represented by Adam and Eve in the allegorical account in Genesis) walked a path of discipline under their teacher, Lord Maitreya. If they had stayed true to him, they would have arrived at the goal of the Tree of Life. Unfortunately, the Serpent (another symbol often used to represent the dweller-on-the-threshold) entered in—and won that round in the ongoing battle of Light and Darkness on planet Earth.

Since then, we have seen mystery schools and spiritual communities come and go: the ancient mystery schools of Atlantis and Lemuria, Pythagoras' community at Crotona, the Knights of the Round Table seeking the Holy Grail, and many others. In this age, Lord Maitreya has established a new mystery school, and he has called his devotees to return to the path they left off long ago. This mystery school is established in a mountain valley in North America's Rocky Mountains, and it is also a worldwide community of students of the ascended masters, those who are studying the mysteries and seeking the Holy Grail.

Another key to overcoming the dweller is the relationship with the master, the spiritual teacher—known in the East as guru. We all know that we can learn from those who have gone before us in any field. But on the spiritual path, this relationship become much more important, for the true master can give of himself to the student, the disciple, the chela. The momentum of the master can truly make the difference (especially in the encounter with the dweller), and while we each must walk the path by our own striving, we need not walk it alone.

The ascended masters are the true teachers, the true gurus of this age. These masters have come from all races and religions. Some we know by name as the great avatars of East and West—those who have ascended to heaven in a pillar of cloud or fire, as Jesus, Zarathustra and Elijah. Some are the great saints who ascended at inner levels after lives of service and devotion. Some are the nameless ones who have simply kept the flame that all might have renewed life and opportunity. Some are great cosmic beings, Elohim and archangels, who come from great heights to assist the evolutions of earth. Collectively, we know them as the Great White Brotherhood—

the ancient name that has not to do with race but recalls the one light out of which all rays and races and religions have come, the white light seen in the aura of the saints. In this and in every age, the ascended masters have sent their messengers to be representatives in delivering their teachings—and their disciplines—to those who seek to walk the Path.

Mark L. Prophet and Elizabeth Clare Prophet are messengers for the ascended masters. For over forty years, they have delivered the teachings of the masters and outlined the path to the ascension. They have given ground-breaking lectures on the enemy within, clearly outlining the anatomy of the dweller and revealing it as the enemy of the soul.

To begin this series of lectures, we introduce you to the ascended master Kuthumi, who delivered this dictation through Elizabeth Clare Prophet. Kuthumi is known as a master psychologist, and he addresses us on this very subject, revealing the psychology of the soul and the dweller. Kuthumi was once embodied as Saint Francis of Assisi, the youth who struggled with his own inner passions to become one of the most beloved saints in the Christian world. In the final embodiment prior to his ascension, he returned as the Eastern adept Koot Hoomi Lal Singh, known as K.H. to students of Theosophy.

Kuthumi has offered to be your personal psychologist, if you will accept him. From the heaven-world, he specializes in helping each one of us overcome the blocks, those things in our personal psychology that trip us up and prevent us from fulfilling our highest potential. May you take his hand, offered in profound love for your soul in the overcoming of the enemy within.

THE EDITORS OF THE SUMMIT LIGHTHOUSE LIBRARY
THE INNER RETREAT
PARADISE VALLEY, MONTANA

CHAPTER ONE

Remember the Ancient Encounter
On Discipleship under Lord Maitreya

Kuthumi

My love enfolds you in a rapturous light of the One Sent. I am, as you know, as you know me, Kuthumi.

Remember the ancient encounter. For I have been your brother on many occasion; and in each succeeding incarnation we have shared, our souls have moved together to pluck the star of the Divine Light and to pluck the harp of the heart of Maitreya.

Disciples of Maitreya are we—Metteyya—and therefore, together we have sought a glance, a smile, a whisper, an acknowledgment that we might know our God is pleased.

Thus, we agreed, thou and I, that I should go with Morya before you to stand in Christ with Jesus and that you would remain to bring up the rear of the troops and your own flaming chakras.

Thus, to play our roles—I the Alpha, you the Omega—we crossed the bar; and you remain, the faithful witness of our cause.

How can I leave thee, devotees of light and peace and freedom and of the heart of that Christ?

Opposition to Our Mission Is Not New

Is it any wonder to you that I should become, not only before my ascension in the final hours [as the Mahatma Koot Hoomi] but subsequently, a bit incensed at these Christians and their small-mindedness and inability to perceive his true mission when I myself [as Saint Francis], through trial and pain and the deep affection of the heart, came truly to understand beyond orthodoxy the Reality of my Saviour?[1]

Thus, beloved, I am impatient today for your sakes and for the sakes of those who wait for the cup of knowledge that you bear from our abode. I am impatient with those who attempt again and again to weave their slander, their unreality and all the rest around such a shining star as the teaching itself.

Of course, I know the end from the beginning. And I, too, understand the cycles that must be outplayed as outlined for you by Sanat Kumara and Gautama and the living Word in the Great White Brotherhood. But still I long to think of those who, if they had the fruit and the sweet nectar of the knowledge that has become such a daily affair as to be taken for granted by yourselves, might run with it, eat it now to the fullness of the cup, and become for us other servants in many fields East and West.

We press on, then. We jump over the bowling balls that are rolled our way, and we stand before you today rejoicing in admonishment and dispensation from Maitreya to our own heart.

My Assignment to Work with You for Your Physical Health and the Healing of Your Psychology

Thus, I come, the joyful student, to announce to you the most precious dispensation, which comes from Maitreya, placed upon me by him with all diligence and the same concern for the step-up of your lives. This dispensation is my assignment to work with each one of you individually for your physical health and for the healing of your psychology, that we might swiftly get to the very cause and core of physical as well as spiritual and emotional conditions that there be no more setbacks or indulgences and surely not two steps forward and one step back.

Thus, from this hour, if you will call to me and make a determination in your heart to transcend the former self, I will tutor you both through your own heart and any messenger I may send your way. Therefore, heed the voices—not astral but physical—and watch the course of events. And of course, when you have the opportunity to receive my word from the messenger, know truly that I use her often to explain to you the intricacies of the blocks in consciousness. For you are so sincere, and the sweetness of thy hearts is touching to the soul in a world hardened by war and abortion.

Thus, I come in many guises. And I do acknowledge to you, beloved, that whatever else may or may not be said from the left or the right, our messenger is truly adequate and ready to demonstrate to you the path of your Christhood as we have walked it, as we have attained it.

A School of Hard Knocks and Our Gruff Voice

This is a school, truly, of hard knocks. This is a school where you will hear our gruff voice. Be of good cheer, for our bark is often worse than our bite but proves most useful in eliminating those who are so easily scared away from the fount, who seek favoritism and praise when, in fact, they should recognize the love of the gruff voice and know that that which is offended is the ego self, the prideful self.

Thus, offense is a grave enemy and ought to be discarded. We use this mode, that those who belong not here may well have their offense and take it and move on their way as the "hurt ones," the "bruised ones," the "injured ones."...

Seek Not the Human Mother but the Divine

Blessed ones, those who come for favoritism and the personality cult, those who come seeking the Mother, therefore, as the substitute for the human mother come precisely for the wrong reason. This is not a human mother! This is the Divine Mother, veiled in many garbs. You cannot have a relationship with the Divine Mother in any of us unless you first satisfy yourself at the human level, resolve your psychology with human parents, become your own mother and father and keeper, and then enter into a true and lasting relationship with the Divine Mother and the Divine Father.

Now, why do you suppose that the good God made human mothers and human fathers? It is because the tender souls, those reincarnating with a pack of karma on their backs, truly need the humanness of the human mother and father. Thus, these are necessary steps in the planetary home, and you would feel bereft and left out if you were spoken of as that one having neither father nor mother nor beginning nor ending of days.[2]

Thus, the one who comes in the name of Melchizedek, the ascended master and the priest, has initiated the Lord Jesus as a priest forever.[3] That priesthood comes through the initiation of the Divine Father and the Divine Mother unto those who have internalized the essential elements of the humanity of the world's greatest fathers and mothers.

I speak, then, of the inner resolution. I speak, then, to you! Those who seek here what they did not derive from human parents, those who seek to prove again and again that human parents will fail by seeing failure in the messengers have not the slightest conception of the Path. Some require tutoring and a study of the true and ancient traditions of the guru-chela relationship.

Blessed ones, we cannot be unto you both human and divine. Therefore, we have chosen—and chosen well—to represent the divine, since you have so many specimens of the human before you. It is really not necessary that we provide the human link in the chain of humanism.

The Ascension Is the Mark of Achievement

We come, therefore, to provide the link to the Divinity, and we place before you in this mystery school the goal of the ascension. The ascension itself is the mark of achievement, the victory and the single act that is praiseworthy. If you do not graduate with your ascension, not only will your report card be marked "failed," but so will ours. For the teacher is also responsible—and so is the messenger.

Thus, each one sent comes with a prayer that none of these little ones should be lost save the son of perdition.[4] And who is the son of perdition? I tell you, he is not the bogeyman! He is not your worst enemy that you imagine to be nine feet tall. The son of perdition is the dweller-on-the-threshold of your own house. It should be lost and rightfully so—and swiftly!

But it is difficult to become a dragon-slayer when the age of chivalry has long passed. Some find it a bit unpleasant to take up sword and slay the not-self. But in the meantime, while their stomachs are in too delicate a condition (and their egos as well) to perform this act, they themselves are being devoured by the dweller—dallying, marking time and often drifting backwards with no realization. For in relativity, it sometimes appears one is going forward when one is standing still or moving backward.

Thus, precious hearts, understand that the ascension is the acceptable offering. Those who do not truly want the ascension but want the power of the light of Serapis Bey ought not to come. But these are the very ones who cannot be convinced to stay away, for they enjoy the lap of the Mother and need make no effort and become most angry when they are sent forth to prove their wisdom in action and thus balance the threefold flame!

They must recognize once and for all that if they had mastery once or twice or thrice in a previous life, that full mastery should have long ago gained for them the eternal octaves of light. What is wanting is always the absence of balance in the threefold flame. If it cannot be gained here, it must be gained in the wide opportunity of the world for professionalism and self-mastery.

Some things are required of one, and some things of another. Resent not, then, the admonishments we give through the messenger. Our admonishments are only for the shortening of the days for the elect.[5] Who are the elect? You are the elect! You have elected to enter a path, in the main, by trust, by determination and by the elimination of possibilities; for you have wisely observed what the world has to offer. Not knowing, then, what you would encounter, you have nevertheless sought the Great White Brotherhood, sought the ascended masters, entered the school presenting itself to be ours (as so it is), and thus come in faith to seek and to find.

I welcome you to this quarter of Summit University in the name of Lord Maitreya. My arms are open, and my heart also. I would take you inside and give to you as much as you are able to take. Thus, enter in to the faith of thy own Self-hood, and we can roll up our sleeves and begin.

"What Does It Mean, This Slaying of the Dweller-on-the-Threshold?"

"What does it mean," you have said, "this slaying of the dweller-on-the-threshold?" Let us begin once again at the beginning for those who have not understood:

Beloved, by free will all have forged action, word, desire. Some of these, as vibration, have been pure and perfect, building individual Christhood and the mantle, the seamless garment. Through ignorance, absence of tutoring, forgetfulness of First Cause and origin in the higher spheres, others of these vibrations emanating from actions and words and desires have fallen; for they had not the balance of flight of Alpha and Omega. They have fallen and begun to form a spiral like a solar system around the solar plexus, the "place of the sun."

Momentums, then, of lifetimes for many thousands of years have builded the antithesis of Self, sometimes entirely unbeknownst to the outer mind who thought itself so sincere and desirous of doing right that in the very desire to do right, there has been the mistaken conclusion that the desire should make all things right. Nevertheless, the Law perceives that there is right action, there is wrong action, and the proof is in the causal body—the pure vessel of light of all good deeds and acts in Matter—and in this electronic belt.[6]

Now, in the eye of that vortex of misqualified energy—in the very eye of the vortex—there is the point of consciousness and identity that emerges as the collective consciousness of all misdeeds. Each time a decision is made that registers as the unreal, a portion of the unreal mind must be used to make it. Thus, the collection of actions has a collective consciousness, and the dweller is the collective manifestation of all that has been in error. It emerges as an identity, a figment, you might say, but a momentum that wields human power to a grave and great extent.

This identity is the impostor of the soul and of the Christ Self. A portion of the soul by free will is invested in the impostor, and a portion of the soul is invested in the Christ. Thus, the battleground and Armageddon is of the soul, which, as you know, can be lost.

Now cometh the Christ and the ascended masters and their chelas to woo the soul away from unreality, to prove to the soul what is Real, what is light, what is the eternal goal. This is your office as shepherds and ministering servants and students of the World Teachers. When the soul is enlightened and quickened and gains awareness through Christ, she* begins to be able to see on her own through that Christ intelligence what is unreal.

But seeing is not necessarily believing. Seeing, then, is the first step; believing, the second.

The action to deny that which is unreal is fraught with the burdens of the individual's psychology. And thus, sometimes hard lessons—burning in the trial by fire,[7] pain in this world— must convince the soul that life is more important and, therefore, that one must let go of certain situations and conditions and beliefs and comfortabilities.

We move the soul as close to the precipice of knowledge

---

* The soul is the feminine counterpart of the masculine Spirit, and thus is referred to using feminine pronouns.

of Absolute Good and Absolute Evil as is possible, at the same time to preserve the integrity of the soul and not to cause that one too much fear, too much awareness of the great Darkness within that opposes the great Light.

Thus, beloved hearts, the slaying of the dweller. Not all at once but little by little. And this is something you should be aware of, though you have been told before. Each day, according to the cosmic cycles, a little bit of the head of the dweller emerges above this dark pool of the electronic belt. It is a still darkness, and one can see perhaps the head or the ear or the eye or the nose of this dweller, this self-created monster. You see this, then, in your own actions and reactions. You see it in the musings of the mind—sometimes only a telltale ripple on the surface or perhaps the tail when the beast has dived to the bottom.

Thus, you must listen and watch what is lurking. And as soon as you find a tendency to fear, to be jealous, to become angry or whatever, go after it as the tip of the iceberg! Work at it! This work is truly a profound work of the Spirit. It is not easy always to be on the path of confrontation.

The Path of Accommodation of the Dweller

I come with the message of Maitreya and to amplify his previous messages. For he has spoken of the path of accommodation* whereby, instead of slaying the dweller, you find ways to go around this side and around that side. And thus, you begin to build the tower of light—you build a great momentum of decrees and service, trusting that somehow, in some way, this terrifying encounter will go away. But it will

---

* *accommodation* (fr. Latin *ad* + *commodare*, to make fit, give, lend): adaptation; adjustment; functional adjustment of an organism to its environment through modification of its habits.

not go away. And the day you discover once again that all of that goodness is not the acceptable offering is the day when, in the presence of Maitreya, you once again encounter face-to-face that dweller-on-the-threshold.

You may go far and wide and keep a wide berth from the messenger and never notice the dweller and build a positive human momentum in those outer attainments, whether through yoga or decrees or this or that discipline. And you may be very happy with yourself, and others may be exceedingly happy with you. Of course, this is not the question.

The question is whether your I AM Presence and Christ Self are happy and whether your teachers will tell you that, in the light of cosmic initiation, your offering is acceptable. Thus, beloved, to avoid the masters or to avoid the instrument whereby we may speak to you is to avoid the day of reckoning of your karmic accountability, which has been called, in biblical terms, the day of vengeance of our God.[8]

Who Is Your God?

Now think of this in the occult* sense. Who is our God? Your God is the thing that you fear most. I pray it be the Almighty in the sense of awe, but too often fear is of things from beneath[9] or of fear itself. Your God is also the thing you hate most or resent most, the thing to which you are tied irrevocably by the greatest intensity of human feelings. These may be good or bad, pleasureful or painful; but there is your God, the one to whom you give deference.

Now listen to the Word: "the day of vengeance of our God." What is the vengeance? It is the terrifying moment

---

* *occult* (fr. Latin *occulere*, to cover up): hidden, requiring more than ordinary perception or knowledge. "We speak the wisdom of God in a mystery, even the hidden wisdom, which God ordained before the world unto our glory..." (1 Cor. 2:7)

when the thing you have feared or hated or loved most (in a human consciousness) has become your master and you its slave, and you find you are indeed not free, although you have built a mountain of decrees and service on either side.

Thus, beloved, the mighty work of the ages must be pursued, and we stand with you and we place our messenger before you because of the initiation and tutoring and training and encounter that is needed constantly to assist—to assist *your* overcoming.

Only you can overcome—we cannot do it for you! And yet, we can deliver the precise Word and the thrust of the sword at any hour of the day or night when it is required. And those who are the true brides of Christ and the wise virgins[10]—*they* will respond, *they* will know the source, *they* will move!

You May Know Us through Our Teachings

Blessed hearts, you may not understand or perceive us personally, but you may do so through the dictations and the teachings. And inasmuch as you never know where you will find it, it is important to be ongoing students of the teachings that have come forth. So precious are these teachings that their recording, their organization, is deemed by us often more important than more human conversation with our messenger.

As you can see, if we did not have our books and letters from previous centuries, where would we be to convey the very same instruction? We would have to begin all over again and repeat what we have done. But we have better and nobler ideas to convey and new situations demanding attention. Thus, do not neglect so great a salvation as the written and spoken Word. And value all other contact above and below with our bands.

The Accommodation of Rebellion against the Guru and Disobedience to the LORD God

Blessed ones, understand, then, the accommodation of the aspect of the beast known as rebellion against the guru and disobedience to the LORD God. Understand that that core rebellion has been the undoing of many chelas, some who were not calculated by us to make it in the first place.

Although we held the immaculate concept, the record of the past was before us. We gave the opportunity in purest hope, in support, and with the full momentum of our Electronic Presence. Yet, beloved, others who have not made it have lost in the race simply for want of this very instruction from Lord Maitreya, which, because it has helped so many, I give to you again.

The accommodation, then, of rebellion, going to the right and to the left of it, becoming as it were, a workaholic, performing many good human deeds and social deeds, or the performance of ritual and prayer and yoga, the assiduous following of perhaps asceticism or personal discipline or diet —all of these things may be a careful accumulation of human virtue by the individual to avoid [subconsciously, at least] what is *the* most important step that must be taken: The step of the encounter with that satellite orbiting in the electronic belt that has come between the soul and her I AM Presence— namely, the rebellion against Lord Maitreya or Sanat Kumara or against the Law itself because it was spoken, perhaps, by a very imperfect vessel. This rebellion, then, becomes a block self-perpetuating, for it is set in orbit by free will and it cannot be removed from orbit without free will.

How You Create Your Personal Astrology
out of Your Karma

When you place planets in orbit in this electronic belt, you create your personal subconscious astrology and psychology, which are one and the same—focuses of your karma. Now, when you think of the solar system you inhabit and you consider the weight, the volume and the magnitude of the planets, you can learn the lesson that it is far easier to set a planet in motion than to call it back, even as the words that proceed from your mouths cannot be called back, no matter how great the regret, else it is by the violet flame.

The Necessity for Attainment in the Heart Chakra
through the Master-Disciple Relationship

Thus, to remove the planet of rebellion, you must have a oneness with the central sun of your being—the I AM Presence, the Christ Self and the externalized attainment of the heart chakra. This is why we preach on the Sacred Heart. This is why there is a union of religion East and West through the path of the heart; for all who have ever attained have done so by this sacred fire.

Listen well, then. To recall the planet of rebellion in the electronic belt, you must have an equal and greater force of light and sacred fire manifest in the heart to counteract it and dissolve it, else you must be holding the hand of the master or the guru who has that development and can transmit to you the light that can keep you above the waves when you would sink as Peter did.[11]

Thus, the necessity of the master-disciple relationship. For there is not one among you or those upon earth today (save those who are already in our inner retreats) who can make it alone, who has not in his electronic belt something that requires reinforcement of the masters who have gone before to remove—to remove, I say, in a timely manner, for we do not have a million years for you to sit and give the violet flame and to pursue these disciplines.

Thus, the master-disciple relationship has never been more important. And because this messenger has submitted to the most complete and arduous training at inner levels and in the physical octave, taking the lessons from both friend and foe alike, from masters and chelas alike (not missing those lessons), we can tell you that the instrument is dependable for our purposes to make known to you what are the mandated options that you must consider through free will to take and take quickly for your own victory.

Cycles must not be lost. Tests must not be postponed. And when you see it, call it and move on.

Beloved ones, when the aspect of the dweller of rebellion is not challenged and bound and cast out—and these are steps; for that planet may be bound before it is ultimately cast out, which means it is in submission to your free will and to your Christhood but not entirely eliminated—when it remains, therefore, and you are in the twilight zone of not having slain the dweller and not having entered into complete union with Christ, these are treacherous waters.

We Offer Our Hand in Friendship

In these waters of the astral plane, again you need our living witness and our hand, which we offer this day purely and in friendship and as never before to assist you—to assist you for Maitreya's sake and for your ascension's sake.

The Acceptable Offering Is Christ-Good

When you are in that twilight zone—scurrying about like frightened mice to pile up good karma, yet not facing the problem—the offering of human righteousness and human goodness is not the acceptable offering. If the individual is not willing to take this teaching to heart and to change, then, you see, he will become angry, as Cain was angry when his offering was not accepted.[12] He demanded of Maitreya that his human goodness be received as a substitute for Christ-goodness—that the Law be changed for him and, instead of his fulfillment of that Law, that all of this grandiose human goodness should suffice.

And individuals do this again and again, and their schemes and their deeds become more and more grandiose, sometimes encompassing the earth. And they say, "Surely this great good deed, this great endowment, this great act I have done that has blessed millions should be the acceptable offering!"

It is only the acceptable offering when it is Christ-good. What is Christ-good? It is the soul united with Christ who has slain the dweller through that Christ and therefore can say, "This I have done to the glory of God and not as an accommodation for my rebellion, not as a substitute for my surrender, not as my demand that God should take me according to *my* path instead of according to His."

Depression and Moodiness for the Rejected Offering

Now when the offering that is not Christ-good is rejected, as it always is and shall be, there is an anger that occurs at the subconscious level, which on the surface may manifest as depression. Beware depression and moodiness, for it is a sign of severe problems. Depression is that state of the twilight zone where the individual has neither slain the dweller nor entered fully into the heart of Christ. It is the most dangerous situation of the soul in this octave of the Matter universe.

Therefore, you desire to quickly remove yourself from that place of jeopardy.

Some of you have recurrent dreams of walking over very insecure bridges, over deep chasms or through narrow passageways, or of being confined in a box. You may wake up in a cold sweat, you may experience terror in the night. And thus, a lesson is coming through from your Higher Mental Body that tells you that you have placed yourself in a condition that is dangerous, that you must pass through it, you must make a move, you cannot go back and you cannot stand still: you must move forward.

Enter the False Gurus Offering Souls False Fruits

For here the tempter may come, here you may be vulnerable to those who are offering you wares and fruits that are not the initiatic fruits of Maitreya.

Thus enter the false gurus to take advantage of souls who have refused to pass through the initiation of challenging that core rebellion. Now they find a false guru, now they satisfy themselves that all is well. They may keep their rebellion, for the false guru is the embodiment of the dweller-on-the-threshold of rebellion against Maitreya. And they will follow the false teachers lifetime after lifetime, totally suppressing all other awareness of the light of Christ.

For that awareness would demand and force them once again to the point of the encounter and the point of the choice. Thus, they have a system of knowledge, of education, of academia—all these things to confirm and hold together a system of civilization based upon pride and the development of the human ego, situation ethics, the modification of behavior, and all that occurs in the molding of the human animal.

Now understand how the individual who ten thousand or twelve thousand years ago in rejecting Maitreya made the conscious decision to keep the dweller of rebellion does react in this hour or in any century when the representatives of Maitreya and the Great White Brotherhood come forth with the true teaching and the true requirements of the Law. Now the anger that is subconscious, that used to manifest outwardly as depression, inverts and is on the surface in an all-out campaign to destroy the society or the organization or the orifice of the true light.

The Soul Holds the Balance of Right Choice, Fortified by Prayer and Meditation

Blessed ones, to a greater or lesser extent, now and then the dweller within you rebels against your own Christhood. But the soul may choose. For the soul ultimately, though it hangs in the balance, holds the balance of right choice. Thus, when you do not know the way to go or the right hand from the left hand, pray—pray for attunement and oneness with us.

Learn the steps of prayer and meditation that we have taught in our release[13] that you might also be fortified by prayer and meditation as the right hand and the left hand of the presence of the bodhisattvas who come to reinforce your desire to be all that God intended you to be.

Thus, you see, depression then begets inefficiency, more rebellion, disobedience, until finally there is a clamoring and a clanking in the electronic belt and in the four lower bodies. And unless that individual swiftly choose the light of his own mighty I AM Presence and choose to align himself with us, the helpers who can help, that individual must surely make the choice to run for the hills or for the canyons of the big cities where he may lose himself and place himself at the farthest possible distance from the one who can help—if not ourselves, then the messenger.

Some Sense of Injustice, Some Offense

Realize, then, beloved hearts, that all who do this must have an excuse, and their excuse must be based on some sense of injustice, some offense, or some real or imagined fault of our witness or our chelas or our organization. It is a pity, beloved hearts, that personal offense based on a core rebellion should unseat the rider, should unhorse the knight and he thereby lose such a grand opportunity. This work of the ages is a joyous work when you have one another, when you have community and such joy unlimited that is possible in this circumstance with which you are blessed, having this center with all that it portends for your lifestream.

We Come in the Name of Serapis Bey because the Mystery School Is Required

Why have we come in this century? Why are we here presenting the equation of life? We come in the name of Serapis Bey, our chief. We come in the name of this master. We come because it is required that there be a mystery school in the physical octave in this century, teaching the path of the ascension, where the only graduates from that school are ascended masters.

It is required that the Path be set, that there not be a mincing of words or indulgences, paid or unpaid,[14] but there be the pure and simple Path demonstrated by ourselves and yourselves to keep this earth in its cosmic spin. We are proud in the true, humble sense of the word as we rejoice that there is indeed such a school in this time and space.

The Messenger of Truth Must Meet
the Foes of the Message

Beloved ones, I must tell you that when we looked for the messenger who could carry this message and Truth through what would befall that messenger in this century, we looked down this lifestream and found that strength and faith that would not be moved by the gossip or the calumny or the framing or whatever else might occur. For if the message is not borne by one who has the strength to meet the foes of the message with their anti-message, then how can our activity or our knowledge endure?

All qualities you may desire may not be evident in the messenger, but can one individual embody all virtues of God? Why are you here? Are you not here to embody those virtues and talents that might be absent from the outpicturing in this life of the one who stands before you? What purpose would you have if it would not be to complement all that is manifest here? What purpose of the messenger if not to provide you with those ingredients necessary and expedient to your own victory? This is the great beauty of the Great White Brotherhood, lest one having more than her share or his share perceive himself a god or independent of the Most High.

Come, then, to understand that the most necessary ingredients—to stand and still stand and to deliver our Word—are present. We are satisfied, and we are also satisfied that you will provide the rest.

Active and Passive Roles of Alpha and Omega
Fulfilling the Word and Its Work

We encourage you to be aggressive and active on those particular notes that are your keynote to make this community complete. You understand the meaning of the passive receiver, the Omega who receives the light of Spirit. The moment you receive it, you become Alpha. And now you are the active ones, now you move into action, now you implement the Word!

Beloved ones, there must be, perforce, workshops drilling in communication. You must be *receivers* of the Word. Then you must be *givers* of the Word. This is not yet action. The Word translated by the Holy Spirit becomes an awareness-action whereby you move. And suddenly the Word, which is the power of the Spirit, becomes the Work, the mighty Work that is the manifestation of the Mother in Matter. This is why we capitalize *Word* and *Work*—that you might understand the polarity of Alpha and Omega.

It is the Omega cycle that you must triumph in. Thus, the Work counts, for it shows forth the effect of the inner cause of the Spirit with you. Until the Word is received and given, heard, assimilated—and the very result of assimilation is the mighty Work of the ages—you have not completed the spiral! And until the Word becomes the Work, it is either an unfulfilled spiral or an aborted spiral.

Great Is the Cry of Injustice, Short-Fused the Determination to Act

I speak of this because I look across this great nation. People meet and talk. They agree in committee. They form policy. If all of the noble thoughts and desires of the hearts of the good people of the land would come into action, this nation would be a highly improved place. But it is not so.

When it comes to the Omega action, when it comes to the individual becoming the Shakti* of the Great White Brother-

---

* *Shakti* is a Sanskrit term for "energy," "power," "force." Shakti is the dynamic, creative force of the universe—the feminine principle of the

hood, when it comes to courage and the willingness to stand apart from the crowd, to go against the most cherished belief systems, we find that those who are often most courageous are the fallen ones, for they have a momentum on rebellion and therefore they stand out.

And those who should stand out are quietly in their living rooms watching their television sets, listening to their music, and demanding endless hours and time to pursue their families and all other interests except the demand to save the nation or the youth or to fight drugs or to rescue the little children.

Great is the cry of injustice, and very short and short-fused is the determination to act. Few have the sustaining power to act in exception to their neighbors for very long. Few can stand the ostracization that they receive. That is why we have community, for we are like minds who ought to be attracting more like minds, and may well do so....

Recapitulation of My Discourse

May I recapitulate and remind you that I have spoken in the beginning of my discourse to you today of the dispensation of my help to you in your personal health and psychology to the end that you might know the joy of wholeness, be at peace to freely and swiftly eliminate the unreal portions of the self, to mount, then, the path of initiation that the flame of the heart might be balanced and shine to all nations as the dissemination of our light, leading all to the fruit of Maitreya and the necessary initiation that every disciple must have if he is to overcome the most difficult and complex problems of the

---

Godhead. In Hindu philosophy, *Shakti* is the name given to the feminine aspect of a male deity, often personified as his spouse or consort. The masculine counterpart is viewed as the quiescent, unmanifest aspect of Spirit, requiring the activating force, the feminine aspect who is Shakti, to release the God potential from Spirit to Matter.

subconscious or the electronic belt.

Our Motive, Our Mode, Our Maitreya

The purpose of all we do is your ascension. Understand that in order to rescue your soul, we must outsmart or challenge or even bruise that dweller. And we must cajole and contrive circumstances where the eyes of the soul will be opened and true self-knowledge will be gained and thus right choices be made. The entire purpose of our instruction at Summit University from the heart of Maitreya is so that you, dear chela, might have at your disposal our standards from the ascended master octaves as you exercise free will for right action—right Word and Work. Understand our motive and tolerate our means, for we must act in the best way possible to reach you swiftly.

Consider always the motive of the ascended masters in any adversity, any clash with a chela or family, any mis-understanding of our teaching or the messenger. Consider the motive and consider that the most important part of any experience you have is not what is flung your way but your reaction to it. Your reaction is the determination of your place on the ladder of attainment. Your reaction enables us to act or not to act. Your reaction to anything or everything shows us the fruit that has ripened in you from all of our prior teaching and loving and support as well as discipline.

Thus, perceive the sine wave building towards events that produce a thrust that requires from you a response. Observe the response, and you will observe the highest hopes and possibilities that now are given room to manifest. It is always well to pause and take a deep breath and to consider, there-fore, before you speak and before you decide on a course of action.

Thus, all is in the pudding. Let us see now the proof of your pudding, for we will not leave thee. We are here for the stated purposes. And we wonder what wonder Maitreya may have before us when you shall have achieved a new level of community attainment.

With the sign of the East and the hierarch of light, with the sign of the One who has sent me, I am forever the little bird of Christ, the little bird of Buddha. I speak in the ear, twitter in the tree, make ripples in the pond, and bring you a little piece of bread in my beak.

CHAPTER TWO

Your Divine Inheritance

Elizabeth Clare Prophet

Each of us has not only a dweller-on-the-threshold, but also a Real Self—the spiritual identity that we are intended to manifest. Understanding this Real Self and contacting that inner light are essential if we are to overcome the dweller.

I would like to give you a unique perspective on your spiritual destiny in the Piscean and Aquarian ages based on your relationship to the Persons of the Trinity and the Divine Mother.

The Chart of Your Divine Self reveals how these four are individualized within you as the Father-Mother God, in the I AM Presence (upper figure); as the Son, in the Holy Christ Self (middle figure); and as the Holy Spirit, who, when you have prepared yourself, may take up his abode in the body temple God provided for your soul's sojourn on planet Earth (lower figure). The Chart shows the fulfillment of the Psalmist's trust:

He that dwelleth [in consciousness] in the secret place of the Most High shall abide under the shadow of

The Chart of Your Divine Self

the Almighty [the mighty I AM Presence].

I will say of the LORD, He is my refuge and my fortress: my God; in him will I trust.[1]

"By This Name I Shall Be Invoked"

God told Moses to tell the children of Israel that his name was I AM THAT I AM and that "I AM hath sent me unto you." Moreover, he said, "Thus shalt thou say unto the children of Israel: The LORD God of your fathers, the God of Abraham, the God of Isaac, and the God of Jacob, hath sent me unto you. This is my name for ever, and this is my memorial unto all generations."[2]

The Jerusalem Bible translates the last sentence: "This is my name for all time; by this name I shall be invoked for all generations to come."

When we call upon the name of the LORD, as the prophets tell us to do,[3] we use the name I AM THAT I AM or simply I AM. Addressing "our God with us" in prayer we say, "Beloved mighty I AM Presence..."

The Almighty, the Maker of heaven and earth, has manifest himself to each one of us as the I AM THAT I AM, who goes before us as the LORD went before the children of Israel, "by day in a pillar of a cloud and by night in a pillar of fire."[4]

The I AM Presence and the seven spheres of light that surround it (the color bands) make up the body of First Cause, or the causal body. These spheres are the many mansions of our Father's house where we lay up for ourselves "treasures in heaven."[5]

Our treasures are our words and works worthy of our Creator, positive thoughts and feelings, our victories for the right, and the virtues we have embodied to the glory of God.

And as Jesus said, where our treasure is, there will our heart be also[6]—in this our heaven-world.

When we judiciously exercise our free will, the energies of God that we harmoniously qualify automatically ascend to our causal body. These energies are deposited in the spheres of light that correspond to the seven chakras and the seven color rays we use in our creative activities. They accrue to our lifestream as "talents," which we may increase as we put them to good use lifetime after lifetime.

John the Beloved saw and described the I AM Presence, calling it a mighty angel: "And I saw another mighty angel come down from heaven, clothed with a cloud: and a rainbow was upon his head, and his face was as it were the sun, and his feet as pillars of fire."[7]

The Multiplication of the Divine Image

The Holy Christ Self is the Mediator between God and man. This Universal Christ is the only begotten Son of the Father—the light-emanation of First Cause. It is the Christ of Jesus and the Christ of you and me. Yet there is but one LORD and one Saviour.

Let us consider for a moment this mystery of the Lord's Body and the Law of the One. The ritual of the breaking of the Bread of Life is the initiation of the individualization of the God flame. Though there be one LORD and one God, yet that LORD and that God has personified himself in the I AM Presence. As depicted in the Chart, the I AM Presence, near and dear, stands just above in direct relation to each of us.

This I AM Presence is the Divine Image of the one LORD and the one God. A thousand or ten billion images of the One still add up to only one LORD and one God in whose light body we all share. One times One times One still equals *the*

One.

In like manner, the only begotten Son of the Father is one Christ and one Saviour. Yet this Son is personified for each child of God in the person of the Holy Christ Self.

Our Father, out of the unfathomable depths of his love for us, has placed the Christ Image of his Son in each of our hearts. A thousand or ten billion images of that One still add up to only one Son of God, one Christ and one Saviour.

Just think of an actual photograph of Jesus being published in *Life* magazine. Ten million copies still add up to only one Jesus.

In giving you and me a mighty I AM Presence and a Holy Christ Self, our Father gave us the Divine Image and the Christ Image—exact replicas of the originals. These Images contain and *are* the Allness of the one LORD and the one God, and the Allness of the only begotten Son, the one Christ and the one Saviour.

Because Jesus Christ is, was and forever shall be the incarnation of the I AM THAT I AM and of the Son of God, he is always one with your mighty I AM Presence and Holy Christ Self. It is this special relationship that you have to the Father and the Son through Jesus Christ that is the foundation of your spiritual destiny in this age.

The True Light

The apostle John penetrated the mystery of the one LORD individualized in the I AM Presence and the one Son and Saviour personified in the Holy Christ Self for every child of God. Thus he wrote of the life that was the Light of men and of John the Baptist, who came to bear witness of that Light.

Of this Light of the I AM THAT I AM and of the Son of God, which are one Light, John proclaimed: "That was the true

Light, which lighteth every man that cometh into the world."[8]

If we do not accept the option "to become the sons of God" through Jesus, our Lord's mission is in vain and so is ours. The mystery of the one Christ individualized and indwelling as seed potential in every child of God is the key of self-knowledge that has been taken away. It is the stone that the builders of orthodox systems have rejected.

They want to make the flesh and blood Jesus "very God of very God"[9] and the only begotten Son of the Father. In truth, Jesus was the Holy Grail in whom the one God and the only begotten Son of the Father dwelt bodily.[10]

Where orthodoxy misses the boat is in its claim of an exclusive divinity and an exclusive sonship for Jesus that denies the God-potential and the Christ-potential to all other souls. It fails to see what John the Beloved saw, that every man (every manifestation of God) that cometh into the world is ignited by the Light of the same God and the same Christ who took up their abode in the temple of Jesus.

The difference between Jesus and the rest of us is that he had the full attainment of that Godhead and that Only Begotten dwelling in him bodily. Inasmuch as we have not yet perfected our Christhood in our souls or in our bodies of flesh, the I AM Presence and the Holy Christ Self dwell above us (not in us) and go before us to light our way.

Jesus' mission was to demonstrate the path of the soul's union with the I AM Presence and the Holy Christ Self. He was the example of that which each of us must one day become. He is our Lord and Saviour because we have strayed far and wide from the house of the Father and the Son, and therefore, without his mediatorship we of ourselves cannot enter into our true relationship with the Father and the Son, as illustrated on the Chart. Nor can we receive our divine inheritance without his grace.

That is why God purposed to send us The Lord Our Righteousness,[11] prophesied by Jeremiah, who would divide the way of Good and Evil within us, teaching us right from wrong. This Lord is indeed the only begotten Son of the Father come to us in the person of our beloved Holy Christ Self. As joint heirs, with Jesus, of the Christ,[12] we are also intended to embody that Christ; for only thus can we sup with him in glory and receive the communion cup of eternal life.

Your Holy Christ Self overshadows you wherever you are and wherever you go. He endows you with the capacity to be "Christ conscious" at all times or, to put it another way, to have the "Christ consciousness" all ways. This beloved friend and teacher and comforter is actually your Real Self, whom you will one day become if you follow in the footsteps of your Saviour.

The Lower Self Becomes the Higher Self

The lower figure is shown enveloped in the violet flame within the tube of light, which descends from the I AM Presence in answer to your call. This cylinder of steely white light sustains a forcefield of protection twenty-four hours a day—so long as you guard your harmony.

Your lower self consists of your soul and your spirit dressed in the garments of the four lower bodies. Your soul is the nonpermanent aspect of being that is evolving through the four planes of Matter. It is made permanent through the ritual of the ascension.

Your spirit is the distilled essence of your self. It is the pervading and predominating presence by which you are known. It is the animating, or vital, principle of your life that you take with you throughout your soul's incarnations, molding it after the likeness of the Spirit of the living God.

The ascension is the culmination of lifetimes of the soul's service to life. The prerequisites for this graduation from earth's schoolroom are (1) the soul must become one with her Holy Christ Self, (2) she must balance at least 51 percent of her karma and (3) she must fulfill her mission on earth according to her divine plan. It is possible for the soul, walking with God, to truly embody the God flame and the God consciousness long before she is called Home in the ritual of the ascension; but not until the hour of her ascension is she fused to the I AM Presence, one forevermore.

Through the ascension the soul is become the Incorruptible One. Henceforth to be known as an ascended master, the soul receives the crown of everlasting life. This is the consummate goal of life, greatly to be desired. The ascension is freedom from the cycles of karma and the rounds of rebirth; it is the entering in to the joy of the Lord.

The Chart is thus a diagram—past, present and future—of your soul's pilgrimage to the Great Central Sun as year upon year up the spiral staircase of initiation you go, drawing nigh to God as he draws nigh to you.[13]

The Gift from Your Divine Parents

The threefold flame of life is your divine spark, the gift of life, liberty and consciousness from your Divine Parents. Also called the Holy Christ Flame, it is the essence of your Reality, your potential for Christhood. It is sealed in the secret chamber of your heart.

The three plumes of the threefold flame are the blue (on your left), the yellow (in the center) and the pink (on your right), corresponding to the primary attributes of power, wisdom and love, respectively. Through the power (of the Father), the wisdom (of the Son) and the love (of the Holy

Spirit) anchored in the threefold flame, your soul exercises her God-given free will to fulfill her reason for being in the physical plane and throughout all time and eternity.

The crystal (or silver) cord[14] is the stream of life that flows from the heart of the I AM Presence to the Holy Christ Self to nourish and sustain the soul and her vehicles of expression in time and space. John saw the crystal cord and described it as "a pure river of water of life, clear as crystal, proceeding out of the throne of God and of the Lamb."[15]

You can think of the crystal cord as an 'umbilical' cord through which the light/energy/consciousness of God flows all the way from the Great Central Sun to child-man embodied on the far-flung planets. It enters the being of man at the crown, giving impetus for the pulsation of the threefold flame as well as the physical heartbeat and all bodily functions.

Shown just above the head of the Holy Christ Self on the Chart is the dove of the Holy Spirit descending from the Father. This signifies that the Comforter attends each life-stream until the soul is spiritually ready to receive the cloven tongues of fire and the baptism of the Holy Spirit.

To that end the son of man, embracing the will of God, matures in Christ Self-awareness as a Christ-filled being day by day. As he gains greater love and greater wisdom as the foundation of his self-mastery, he enters into true communion with his Holy Christ Self.

In due course, when the alchemical marriage of the soul to the Holy Christ Self is fully accomplished, the Holy Spirit will come to him and he may hear the approbation of the Father: "This is my beloved Son in whom I AM well pleased,"[16] testifying that the son of man has become the sacred vessel of the Son of God. He is now ready to begin his mission in Christ as the servant of his Lord.

The Divine Mother, the Sacred Fire and the Chakras

The Divine Mother is focused and adored in the temple of man through the sacred fire that rises as a veritable fountain of light from the base-of-the-spine chakra to the crown chakra. The seven chakras are the spiritual centers in the body that distribute the light of the Mother ascending from the base of the spine, and the light of the Father descending from the I AM Presence.

The coming together of these two radiant streams of life energy, pulsating from above and below, establishes the union and the balance of the plus-minus (yang-yin) forces in the chakras. Thus each chakra becomes a center for the release of the light of the Father-Mother God. Each focuses one of the seven color rays and one of the seven planes of being.

In the spiritually developed, the Mother's sacred fire (known in the East as the Kundalini) rises up the spinal stalk for the quickening of the soul and the awakening of the Inner Christ and the Inner Buddha. Our Divine Mother, ever present with us, guards and guides our footsteps, teaching us how to attain our self-mastery by taking command of our soul and our spirit, our four lower bodies, and the sacred fire that we release through our chakras.

The Four Lower Bodies

The four lower bodies are four energy fields. They are interpenetrating sheaths of consciousness, each vibrating in its own dimension. And so you have a flesh and blood body that is your physical body. You have a mind that cogitates, which is your mental body. You have emotions and feelings, which express through your astral, or desire, body (also called the emotional body). And you have a memory that is housed in your etheric, or memory, body, the highest vibrating of the four, which also serves as "the envelope of the soul."

These four lower bodies surround the soul and are her vehicles of expression in the material world of form. The planets also have four lower "bodies" demarcating the etheric, mental, astral and physical planes in which their evolutions live and evolve. These four quadrants of being correspond to the fire, air, water and earth of the ancient alchemists.

Our four lower bodies are intended to function as an integrated unit like "wheels within wheels." Or you might think of them as interpenetrating colanders. When the "holes" are lined up, your four lower bodies are in sync. This means they are aligned with the blueprint of your lifestream that is sustained by your Holy Christ Self, enabling you to direct the light through your chakras without obstruction to bless and heal all life.

But most of us don't have our "holes" lined up. We're out of alignment with our Real Self, and so we don't experience the full benefit of our just portion of the light that descends over the crystal cord from our mighty I AM Presence.

The problem we have to deal with if we are to emerge from earth's schoolroom as an integrated personality in God is this: During our stay on this planet we have gotten our spiritual pores clogged up with a lot of human karma and astral effluvia (i.e., the dust and debris of the misqualified energy of the centuries). In addition, each of us is carrying a percentage of the total planetary karma in our four lower bodies.

As we have misqualified God's pure life stream perpetually flowing from our I AM Presence for our use here below, it has accumulated in the subconscious as rings on our tree of life and in the collective unconscious of the race. Like it or not, we are bearing one another's karmic burden, simply because we are a part of this evolution. And that, too, is our karma!

Apropos this, we saw a graphic representation of how negative energy can accumulate in the 1989 comedy *Ghostbusters II*. At the beginning of the film, the "ghostbusters" discover a river of pink-orange slime flowing in an abandoned Manhattan subway tunnel. They determine that the slime is the materialization of negative human emotions—hate, violence and anger. The slime begins to grow and multiply, gathering momentum in response to the population's continued output of negative energy; it starts pushing up through sidewalks, threatening to envelop the city and inaugurate a "season of evil." It can be counteracted only by positive energy—peace, love and good feelings.

In order to galvanize the positive energy of New Yorkers, the ghostbusters positively charge the Statue of Liberty, which comes to life and wades into Manhattan. People come out in the streets and cheer. The slime is finally overcome when the crowd sings "Auld Lang Syne."

Although we don't take it too seriously, this movie illustrates what those who are sensitive have always known: the negative energy we put out attracts more of its kind and by and by returns to overtake us unless we seek and find resolution. And sooner or later the astral slime spills over into the physical plane and the mist becomes the crystal.

The Accumulation of Our Karma

As we near the end of the age of Pisces, we are reaping the karma of that 2,000-year cycle as well as previous cycles. In the days of Noah, God, through nature, cleared the planetary computer, though not entirely, in the sinking of Atlantis, otherwise known as the Flood. Our karma has been accumulating not only since the Flood but also since the end of the last age of Pisces, 25,800 years ago.

Karma is not intended as punishment, although those on the receiving end of it may experience it as such. Karma is intended to teach us life's lessons we have refused to learn in any other way. Karma is the effect of whatever thoughts, feelings, words and deeds we have set in motion through our freewill qualification of God's energy.

By returning to us exactly what we put out, the Great Law, as Proverbs says, forces the fool to return to his folly as the dog returns to his vomit.[17] This return of the soul to her karmic condition may recur "seventy times seven"[18] or until the lesson is learned and we go and "make karma no more."

Most of us have set in motion good causes that have produced a harvest of good effects (very good karma!), which, as I said, are stored in our causal body. But we have also been putting out negative energy, and we have reencountered it as it has come full circle after gathering more of its kind, multiplying and being multiplied by negative world momentums. And we've been putting it out for a long time. Too long.

Often we have sown error unwittingly, witlessly, in ignorance of cosmic law; and we must admit that sometimes we have wittingly, witfully directed harm toward other parts of life. And now the Great Law requires us to pay the price for our unknowing wrongs as well as for our willful wrongdoings.

The message of the transition between two ages, Pisces and Aquarius, is this: We must pay our karmic debts.

Nevertheless, by the grace of our Lord we may pray, "Father, forgive us our trespasses against the law of thy bountiful love, even as we do wholeheartedly, unreservedly forgive those who have trespassed against us"[19] and thereby truly know salvation through the mercy of God.

The Power to Become Sons of God

The reason Jesus came to demonstrate the path of personal Christhood was so that the children of the light could follow in his footsteps throughout the Piscean age and beyond. And therefore, he saw to it that it was a path that they could walk and work.

But the knowledge of this path was not preserved for them by Church or State. Having had no teachers to teach them the Christian mysteries that Jesus imparted to his disciples, the children of the light have missed the point of their soul's true calling from God to walk and work this path that our Lord taught by example.

It was God's grand design that his children fulfill this calling to a personal Christhood in the Piscean dispensation. Therefore he sent his Son Jesus Christ to empower them "to become the sons of God." John the Beloved inscribed this, the greatest promise of the greatest grace of all time and space:

> He came unto his own, and his own received him not. But as many as received him, to them gave he power to become the sons of God, even to them that believe on his name: which were born not of blood, nor of the will of the flesh, nor of the will of man, but of God.[20]

God gave us this promise because many, by sins against the Holy Trinity and the Divine Mother, had allowed the divine spark, the gift of God-identity in the beginning, to be extinguished and thereby had also lost their connection to the Holy Christ Self.

Therefore, for all who would work out their own salvation "with fear and trembling,"[21] as Paul admonished the followers of Christ at Philippi to do, God sent his Son Jesus Christ to rekindle their threefold flame and to reestablish the tie to their Holy Christ Self.

What this promise recorded by John means is that if those who are without the divine spark will receive Jesus Christ as their Lord and Saviour, believing "on his name" and accepting him as the Great Exemplar of the course that they themselves must now run, the Son of God will reignite their threefold flame, thereby giving them a second chance "to become the sons of God"—a second chance to bless the tie that will now bind them to their Holy Christ Self.

The restoration of this eternal flame is the salvation that the Son of God offers to a world that comprehends not the Light because it abides in its own Darkness.[22] Wherefore "the Word was made flesh and dwelt among us (and we beheld his glory, the glory as of the only begotten of the Father), full of grace and truth."

The threefold flame and the Holy Christ Self are the means whereby every living soul who came forth from God may return to him by the path of personal Christhood—the path of words and works multiplied by the grace of Jesus Christ. This is our calling from God, beloved. It is his call to our souls to return to the altar of the Temple Beautiful in heaven. And this is the altar call that we can and must answer at this crossroads of the centuries.

The path of personal Christhood is not the beaten path, though it should be. For the wolves in sheep's clothing,[23] the embodied fallen angels who have positioned themselves in Church and State, have taken away the body of our Lord's teachings and the blood of his sacred mysteries.

Why? Because they fear that the children of the light, lawfully exercising the threefold flame of the Father, the Son and the Holy Spirit, will rise to the stature of full joint-heirship with the eternal Christ. And then these children of the light just might, in the name Jesus Christ and in the name of their own Holy Christ Self, rise up and overcome these reincarnated money changers and cast them out of the temples of God and man!

And so the children of the light are as shorn lambs— scattered sheep whose shepherd the Evil One did smite.[24] They are ill-equipped for their mission in this new age of Aquarius because they do not have either the awareness of the enemy or the fullness of the self-knowledge (what the early Christians called *gnosis*) of the Universal Christ indwelling.

It is time to revisit the temples of ancient Atlantis where we find inscribed upon the walls: "Man, know thyself!" and "Man, know thy self as God!" Nor should we forget the words of Moses quoted by Jesus: "I have said, ye are gods; and all of you are sons of the Most High."[25] Therefore, O man, know the enemy within and the enemy without, who would take from thee the great truth of thy divinity.

CHAPTER THREE

The Creature That Was, That Is, and That Is to Come

Mark L. Prophet

God is many things to many people, so that we can well say that God is made in the image of man, rather than man is made in the image of God, because many people have different concepts of God. You don't have to think long or hard to realize this.

Some envisage God as being a wrathful old gentleman, who sits there watching every move to see if you'll steal the pie on the windowsill while it's still warm, or if you'll wait till it's cold, and he'll punish you for either one. Some imagine God as sitting apart like a great king in a throne room, with all of the angels and archangels bowing to him and saying, "How great thou art." Some people imagine God as Henry Van Dyke did, as coming down to dwell with the people who work. They imagine God as a humble old gentleman, who might even walk around the earth some time or other, or an elderly lady who might hobble around here and there with a benign look upon her face. They, of course, see God in a pantheistic concept. They see God as everywhere, and yet as nowhere in particular, and perhaps *in* people—some people but not in all people, at least not manifest in all people.

These are different concepts. I'm not saying to you that these are right concepts. They may be right in part. But I'm pointing out that many people have a God made in their own image.

Is it not unquestionably true that there is a God made in *his* own image? Is it not true that there is an Absolute? Is it not true that the Creator is that Absolute, and that it is up to us to conform to his intents and purposes? Is it not a simple thing for us to realize that God who has this great wisdom must, of course, in his higher knowledge have a better way of life for us than we could have for ourselves? Therefore, would it not be the part of wisdom, the better part of valor, the best part of all discretion, to submit to his holy will?

Many Unconsciously Recoil from the Will of God

Thomas Aquinas pointed out some of these factors, and Thomas à Kempis in his *Imitation of Christ,* and our own beloved Morya, who, in his many releases, has stated that the will of God is good.

I think it goes without saying that many people unconsciously recoil from the will of God. It is almost the strange sophistry of the human mind that goes out into the schoolyard, and because the individual is athletic and possessed with athletic prowess and great capability, scorns being a Boy Scout and thinks that everyone who has the Eagle Scout badge of honor or some of the various merit badges of the Boy Scouts of America is a sissy. It is almost this way with a lot of people and God Almighty. They seem to think that their own way is the best way, and that God's way is perhaps a bit too much a tinhorn saint. These have not understood God.

And if you, yourselves, will stop to think about it very carefully, you will realize that God and his will are so perfect an image of blessedness for everyone on earth who will partake of it, that we should, so to speak, gobble up all we can get of God's will and God's knowledge and God's light and everything that God can do and will do for us.

We should not permit ourselves to be deceived by the miasma of the world. And the world is full of it. They're full of opinions about religious people. And these subtle opinions have an insidious way of creeping into our mind, at times, and causing us to reject that which we ought to accept for our own soul's salvation.

The Razor's Edge

One of the pitfalls on the path of acceptance of the will of God that troubles many people is the fact that as they begin to accept the will of God more and more, they begin to identify with it. And as they identify with it, there is a certain point on this razor's edge of the will of God and the will of man whereby we seem to feel that we are just a little bit better than those who do not identify with the will of God.

Now here is the subtle part of it. If you say you are not, what then? If you are not any better than they are, then you have brought yourself down to the point where you're denying the Lord that brought you. And if you say that you are better, then you are questionably exalting yourself.

Now this is a very subtle point, but one that will bear interest, if you will try to understand it. When you come to that point—a point prior to complete identification with God in all of your many facets of being—where you can prefer in honor the will of God, you come to a point where you can seek it. But you must be careful that this honored prize does not become self-righteousness, so that you begin to feel that you are better than others. You must always transfer your feelings to the Godhead—and this is the way of escape out of this pitfall.

When you claim "I AM *THAT* I AM," you are claiming God. And when you claim God, you are no longer identifying with the human. You're claiming that you are that I AM. And that I AM is not puffed up, and doth not behave itself unseemly.[1] So when you act as God, you have the compassion for the sinner and the ungodly, for the wretched and the miserable, for those who need your assistance. And you need no longer hold yourself back from the highest manifestation of God through this delusion that you might become exalted. You must recognize that through identification with God, you are doing the Father's will and you are in your rightful place and no one can take it from you.

The Beast That Was, That Is, and That Is to Come

This is a great mystery; it is the mystery of the beast that was, that is and that is to come. This is transcendentalism. The beast that was, of course, is the first primitive manifestation of evolutionary man. The beast that is, is the manifestation you currently wear. And the beast that is to come is the transmuted image, where the bestiality is actually weeded out of the nature and the Divine manifests.

The only reason we use the term *beast* at all is because we are dealing here with a creature. So because using the word *beast* confuses the issue with many people, it would be better to say the creature that was, the creature that is, and the creature that is to come. Because God did not create, although mankind seem to feel that he did, the animal forms presently embodying the earth. He created man in his own image.

When we read the lofty statements in Genesis, which mankind today in their modern theology (and I know also in the past) have interpreted to mean that God had created all the creeping things of the field and the crawling things, we find certain questions arising in our mind as to why God would create a mosquito or a fly or a bumblebee or a devouring animal. And we find, then, compressed within the pages of Genesis, a history of the divine creation and a history of the divine creation through divine men—and then, subsequently, a creation through divine men who fell from their divinity yet retained their powers to create and acted to create until their powers were curbed.

Now our modern theology and our orthodox Church, our orthodox Christianity that is in the world today, would reject this as totally unacceptable to them. Yet they cannot accept their own theology; they cannot accept that which they themselves believe, or profess to believe.

We speak the truth of this matter, because we have been able to go back into the akashic records* and perceive how this creation was done. It was a simple matter, if we understand that among the qualities that God conveyed to man was the quality of creating, or being a creator. In other words, man the created was endowed with the power to create. And it is through the power to create that men wrought evil, because their thoughts were evil—"As a man thinketh in his heart..."[2]

God Conceives Only of Perfection

Heaven, of course, in its simplicity and purity, in the holiness of the divine concept, could never have conceived of

---

* Akasha is primary substance, the subtlest, ethereal essence, which fills the whole of space; "etheric" energy vibrating at a certain frequency so as to absorb, or record, all of the impressions of life. The akashic records can be read by adepts or those whose soul faculties are developed.

evil. Heaven, in its own perfection and absoluteness, could not have comprehended a dimension of evil. Therefore, God did not, in all of his knowing, have knowledge of man's frailty.

Now this would appear to us to make the Godhead possessed of naïveté, as though God himself were a simple child who did not comprehend possibilities that you and I can see. But not so, when rightly understood.

The Godhead is so enamored with the transcendence of divine perfection that the Godhead could not possibly enter into a vibratory action so far below the lofty ideals that God must hold in order to be God. But man—*the created creator*—being engaged in a state of form, maneuvering with form and substance as the lower manifestation, could very easily conceive of the possibility of a fall. And I think that one of the greatest and cleverest tools among all that the so-called devil holds in his little toolbox is the concept that "you might some day fall."

Fear of the Fall

People have found that children who are not subjected to the idea of fear are often able to walk a tightrope at a very early age. I do not think that all babies are this way, and I do not say that I would suggest that you try it for babies, but there are some who are able to have no fear at all, and they will therefore do things that those who have fear will not do.

The question of fear and its value has been often discussed. And we realize that it is good that we do have fear of some things: for "the fear of the LORD is the beginning of wisdom," and it is well that we be reminded from time to time of the possibilities, of the things that could happen to us, if we did not follow divine precepts and common sense.

For example, if instead of crossing a bridge on the

footpath provided for us by the engineers, we would walk the railing, which might be two or three inches wide, we would find, of course, that many people would lose their balance and fall down and be killed. So it is a better part of wisdom to walk the footpath and to follow the traffic laws of our land. But this, too, has many aspects, many facets.

This fear of spiritual fall is one, of course, that is not lacking in validity, because we know that Judas Iscariot fell, and we know that Peter denied our Lord, and we know that many very noble men and women in the past have fallen. So the enemy finds a great deal of ammunition to bring to our attention to say, "You might fall. You might slide back. You might not make it."

Faith Must Overcome Fear

Here is where the deployment of faith must override the concept of fear. Here is where the hand must be thrust into the Father's hand. When this comes about, what must you do in order to achieve and retain spiritual victory and prevent yourself from being victimized by these projected thoughts of the enemy?

You must do this. You must first of all deny that power in your own life by saying, "You have no power in my world. You have no power in my life. My life is in the hands of God." And then having denied it, you must place yourself in a consciousness in the hands of God—*in consciousness in the hands of God.*

You must consciously say, "Father, into thy hands I commend my life! You are my victory! I AM victory! I AM he that overcometh the world!" And once again you identify with the infinite Spirit. You must not, under any condition, in dealing with spiritual matters, accept the idea that you can fall. But you must be extremely careful that no vanity and conceit mar your life at that point.

At that moment when the tempter comes and says to you, "You might fall," you must not then reference your personal life up to that point and say, "This is not true, for I have overcome much already." You must not say, "Why, look at my life and my record. I started out as a vile sinner. I began to seek God when I was so old. I have never fallen off of this pedestal," or "I've fallen, but I've always overcome."

Do not lean upon the arm of your flesh, or upon anyone's flesh, when the tempter comes. Because if he can get you to lean upon your own arm of flesh and say to yourself, "Well, look at my record," he has raised you up egotistically. And then, watch out, because he will come again and say, "You might fall." And then, of course, you might, just in order to prove to you that you had been leaning upon your own flesh and not upon the arm of God. So the thing to do is to deny him power and to affirm God's power to keep you. And thus, he that does not slumber, he that does not sleep, will keep you.[3]

An Internal Battle

Now strange as it may seem to you, the battle for perfection goes on within the arena of your own self, within your own mind and heart. And temptations come to you right where you are. You cannot escape those temptations. You could go to the ends of the earth, but the temptations would follow you, because they are a part of the test—and man is tested. Therefore, it may be well that you understand a little of the meaning of the dweller-on-the-threshold.

When you first came forth from the Godhead into the world of form, you had a clean, white record. You did not have, as Freud pointed out, a subconscious mind, because there were no impressions stored there. Or if there were any, they were the impressions of the Godhead concerning the mastery of all energy and all substance.

You might have a memory of being able to think yourself into the air, and you would rise. You might have a memory of being able to pass through walls or substance, or look down into the earth with the power of a Superman. You might have a memory of being able to flash your thoughts to the farthest star and bless the people there and feel the people gather there in the town squares and send back waves of love to you. You might have a memory of an ancient civilization or an ancient perfection in God. You might have the cosmic memory of the Godhead manifesting in you when you first took embodiment. But you might not have been able to retain the sequential relationship of that memory, and therefore it would lack a coherent concept, for yourself. In other words, it would seem too dim to bring into the reality of yourself, and therefore you probably would reject it as having no real meaning—being perhaps a ghost, a phantom, a fleeting thought. But this would be the cosmic mind, the infinite mind, God, holding the cosmic memory of creation aeons ago, perhaps, shall we say, from the beginning—although there is no beginning, there is no ending, there are only the cycles—but you would be able to cycle back as far as you could go, and then that would be the periphery, the reach of your being into the past. But this would have no meaning to you, you see.

The Accumulation of Records in the Subconscious

Now you come, and you as an entity, as an individual, are born, and you begin to store in the subconscious mind various pieces of knowledge—of your environment, of the happenings to you over a period of years and then embodiments. This constitutes for you a subconscious being. In that subconscious being, not only are there elements of love and elements of greatness, practicality, manifestation of ability to comprehend great things and to master Matter, materia, but there is also stored there the memory of hurt, hurt thrown from the hand of another, hurt inflicted by you upon another.

With the passing of centuries, this becomes quite a record. People who keep a diary know that in the course of a lifetime—or even one year written down three hundred and sixty-five days in a little diary—this record can make quite a bit of reading. Some of these events, if they were recorded— and they often are not, because people wish to forget them— would be pretty dark and pretty sordid in a lot of people. They've had many shames in their past lives and also in this one.

This, then, en masse, put all together in one volume, becomes a dweller-on-the-threshold. And most men and women have probably manifested more evil—or intervals of absence from either good or evil, which goes to the negative. The aspects of good are stored in the causal body, but the interring within the bones of man of the evil manifestation constitutes the dweller-on-the-threshold.

Many people prefer now, at this point, to play the ostrich. They wish to keep their head buried in the sand so that they cannot see. They wish to say, "I cannot look." And so Nature in her great manifestation of mercy hides from man these nether-world aspects of himself, within his own being.

But when he starts out on the path toward God, there comes a point when these energies must be brought before himself for redemption, for judgment. This is the last judgment for the individual, in a sense of the word, because this energy must be released or it will be the oppressor of man's lifestream, and it will effectively bar him from the gates of heaven.

Therefore, when they start out, many people find that they suffer more adversity as they get closer to the throne of grace than they ever did before, simply because they were always saying, "I don't want to pay it. I don't want to pay it. Let it go. Ah, Our Father, please hold back my karma, because it's too heavy for me. I just can't handle any more than I have right now, and I want to be good. So if you'll only give me a few more years to live on this earth, I'll be good, or I'll do this or I'll do that."

And these broken promises—and they usually are broken —cause the day of payment to be put off, and the dweller gets bigger and bigger and bigger.

Facing the Dweller

So the dweller-on-the-threshold, for many people, has become as huge as this Gargantua, the gorilla,[4] or Godzilla, or one of these creatures from the minds of the moviemakers. This huge gorilla form consists of all the greedy, grasping, humanistic—not divine now, and I'm not talking about humanitarian, but humanistic in the sense that it typifies carnal man—all these greedy appetites form this gorilla. And when people come to the point where they face the dweller-on-the-threshold of their own being, some have fled in terror and have left—just gone off and turned their back on it. They wouldn't have anything to do with it.

But this energy must be consumed and transmuted. All of the precious energy in that form must be released and sent back to the Great Central Sun. This material, this substance, is spiritual energy trapped there in this gorilla form, or in this animalistic form. I only use gorilla because it is often true that this will be a gorilla. A lot of people find that it is. It's huge; it may even come at you like that. But it's your own creation that you've made.

Now there are very few people who will tell you this, because they don't want to frighten you. And I don't want you frightened. But I realize that the day will come when you may face this dweller-on-the-threshold. And when you do, you must have the power within yourself to be able to cope with him, to master him, to slay the dragon, this fire-breathing creature that will come out of the pit of your own past delusions for justification, for release.

When you are free of that form, and all other forms like it, you can then say with Jesus, "The prince of this world cometh and findeth nothing in me"[5]; because all that substance will be transmuted and you will be as pure as you were when you first came forth from the heart of God. But the difference, now, is that you will have a mind capable of comprehending self.

When you first came forth from God, all you had was the God-mind. You only had the God-being to manifest. Now you have developed self, and you have separated from self the base elements. And what has now come to the surface, into full view, is the golden moments of the golden man. This is the Christ individuality, the emanation of the Father perfected through form and victory. This is resurrection, and it is readiness for ascension—resurrection because you are resurrected out of the dead works, the works of the dead.

You may as well understand that the statement in the Bible, "to judge the quick and the dead,"[6] references the world today, who are dead in their trespasses and sins, and the quick, those who are quickened in consciousness by the Christ image. This does not separate you from that. In other words, just simply because you are divine and you are divinely quickened, does not mean that you have no longer a sense of responsibility. So long as you are on earth, your responsibility is to manifest the will of God.

Mastery of Self Is the Goal

So let your devotion be to what the divine intent is, and love that image into manifestation. Let that flame burst forth on the altar of your heart. This is the meaning of devotion, not simply adoration that develops a good feeling, that makes you content and happy, but devotion to the first cause that is your freedom. This is mastery, this is true self-mastery. This is what God intends. And it is in the mastery of the subtleties of life that you become master of self. Unless you do, you are no different than the Pharisees and the Scribes: they too sit in worship, they too listen to beautiful music, they too sing. There is nothing that goes on here, practically, that does not go on elsewhere in some form or another.

The difference, then, must be in the manifestation of the character of God, the character of good, the creation, the creative fire, the fire of creation. It is the transmutation of man. And when the transmutative effort has reached up until it has contacted the hem of the garment of the Lord, like the woman who crept behind Jesus with an issue of blood that would not dry up, you will find that you will be made whole by this grace that comes to you through devotion—but not just devotion to anything, but devotion to the Supreme One.

Let us, then, in all of our services learn the meaning of the mastery of self and the pouring forth of devotion to the real Eternal God, whose immaculate concept created every master who has ever lived and walked this earth, who has manifested the sacred fire, who has been able to pour out the power of God. These masters have contacted Reality; it was not imagination, as is the case of many people.

So just remember, dear hearts, that the vision is an interior vision. And if there is anything in the world that I could convey to you this morning in closing this little talk, it is the meaning of the interior vision, of being able to see God as opportunity each day to make progress in outpicturing his image and his likeness. His image and his likeness is not the image of Mark, or the image of Alex, or of Tom, Bill, nor Sigrid, nor Anita, nor Ruth—it's not anyone's image, it's the image of God. And in this similitude, we are one. It is no desecration to impute this to ourselves. This is our birthright, this is why we came here: to master it down here.

This Plane Is Where We Must Win Our Victory

Up there you're like a flame in a sea of fire. Down here you have band-spread. There is enough space down here where we can live apart from one another. And in this band-spread, this expansiveness of space and time, this continuum of space and time, we are given opportunities that would be impossible if we were in the higher octaves. This is the battleground; this is the place where God is laid, in this manger, the manger of human substance. And it is here that we win our victory.

We must be face-to-face with our self. In heaven there could not remain one vestige of our self. If we were taken now and transported there this instant, everything that we have made that is not God would end like that, in the twinkling of an eye. It would be changed. And those of us who did not have enough of God developed would be without hands or feet or head or form. We would be lacking, we would be incomplete, our identity gone.

And so we are down here in order to develop identity in all of our parts, in all of our members. We're here to develop spiritual hands, spiritual hearts, spiritual heads, spiritual necks that are not stiff, spiritual limbs and a spiritual body. And when we do it in the interior of ourselves, then it does not matter what the outer self looks like. Because the outer self must conform to that which is within.

It is only a question of time until the manifestation of this fire body will mold and shape and vulcanize the outer self, the identity, the total man, until in the twinkling of an eye he is caught up to heaven in a chariot of fire, as Elijah was. He goes roaring up to God because he is like God—but he retains for all eternity the individuality of himself, a transmuted self, a worthy self, a divine self. This is the plan, the purpose, cause-and-effect relationship.

"When He Shall Appear, We Shall Be Like Him"

You are not the First Cause, but you are *a* cause. The First Cause is God. He provided opportunity. The second cause is you. You provide the second opportunity.

The first Adam is of the earth, earthy. The second Adam is the Lord from heaven. As you have worn the image of the earthly, so you shall also wear the image of the heavenly. "And it doth not yet appear what we shall be: but we know that, when he shall appear, we shall be like him; for we shall see him as he is."[7] Vision, then, is important.

And I say to you, hold your heart's altar as the altar of devotion, the place where God is. And as his votaries, when you pray, when you are devoted, invoke, convoke the flame of God there. And let that flame expand. This then immortalizes substances, changes ideas and makes wholly perfect the Divine Son, who then becomes one with God.

CHAPTER FOUR

Archetypes of the Dweller

Elizabeth Clare Prophet

One of the challenges we face in dealing with the dweller is to recognize it. The dweller seeks to hide, to masquerade, to blend in with the furniture of our own mental and emotional bodies. Therefore, we have a problem: How do we identify something we have never seen clearly? One approach to this dilemma is through the analysis of archetypes of the dweller that have been portrayed in literature and popular culture. Having seen the dweller objectified, it then becomes easier to recognize elements of its consciousness lurking in our own being.

The encounter with the dweller-on-the-threshold has been vividly portrayed in some classic works of literature. The nineteenth century English novelist and mystic Sir Bulwer-Lytton in his novel *Zanoni* describes the encounter of an initiate on the Path with "the dweller of the threshold" whom he secretly invokes in his teacher's laboratory while the adept is away. In this case, the dweller is depicted as a hateful, mocking female, almost reptilian in form, who seeks to drag him into her cold embrace.[1]

Thereafter, throughout the rest of his life, as long as he indulges his lower nature, the dweller is appeased and does not appear to him, but whenever he tries to rise above that level, she reappears to haunt him.

Frankenstein

The novel *Frankenstein* written in 1817 by Mary Shelley, the wife of Percy Shelley, also illustrates the fateful encounter with the dweller. In this case, the mad Dr. Frankenstein creates a living creature reminiscent of the *golem* of Jewish folklore. The golem was a robot-like servant created out of clay and brought to life by pronouncing the sacred name of God over its form.

The dweller is like the Frankenstein monster and like the robots created by the fallen angels. The fallen angels are not content, therefore, to aid and abet the soul in creating the not-self. They also create mechanization man, robot creations, who are then ensouled by demoniac spirits who will torment the soul from without as well as from within.[2]

Once the Frankenstein monster is given life, once the pride of the creator has allowed him to pass to the monster the sacred name of God, then the monster gains power over its creator and eventually turns on him in revenge. In the same way, when we use the name of God, I AM, to create our negative self, that is how we empower that self. When we say "I am sick, I am weary," or say to another: "You are evil. You are hateful," we are taking the light of God to create that Frankenstein monster.

Descending, then, into the electronic belt, the soul, unaccompanied by Archangel Michael, is not able to overcome that dweller. The dweller is angry because it is not a living soul, it is not the issue of God, and yet it contains a portion of the power of God by having received his name when the creator created that robot.

The descent into the Death and Hell of the planetary body by the lightbearers must therefore be accompanied by the hosts of the Lord Archangel Michael. And without Archangel Michael, we are not able to subdue either the counterfeiting spirit or the planetary collective unconscious, the planetary dweller-on-the-threshold, which is the combined dweller of all of the negative karma or evil from all people living upon earth.

That combined dweller manifests as a false hierarchy of fallen angels who have vowed to embody evil, who have taken the left-handed path. And rather than be overcome by the Sons of God, they will first make war, nuclear war. They will first destroy the bastions of his dwelling place, the economy. They will first wreak havoc in the environment, destroy the ecology, bring about pollution, create plague, premeditated viruses put in the community, such as AIDS. They will move against the lightbearers rather than be devoured by the sacred fire. This is the true meaning of Armageddon. This we must remember.

Will the dweller-on-the-threshold of any one of us or of the planet overcome the souls of the lightbearers before they can be rescued, before the light can dawn upon them and they can know the Lord face to face and be like him?

There is only one answer to this question: Lightbearers must determine to put the capstone on the pyramid of civilization. Lightbearers must raise up the All-Seeing Eye of God. If you are one of the components of the capstone, you must know this: that to enter that capstone and be a cell in that All-Seeing Eye of God, raising up the ensign of God in the people, you must have overcome your dweller and seen to it that it is bound. As long as the dweller is bound by Archangel Michael in answer to your calls daily, he is bound until the day when the violet flame and the sacred fire will utterly consume the cause, effect, record and memory of that dweller.

So long as there is karma, there will be a vestige of the consciousness of karma, which is the dweller. But so long as you invoke daily the person of Archangel Michael, that dweller will remain bound within you. And when it is bound, you can join Archangel Michael for the meeting of that adversary against our nation, our freedom and our defense.

There is no room for the dweller in the capstone of the pyramid. It is too small. There is only room for the soul in light. There is room for a billion souls in light in the capstone. There is not room for one dweller.

Dr. Jeckyl and Mr. Hyde

Another very instructive portrayal of the dweller-on-the-threshold at its worst is contained in Robert Louis Stevenson's famous novel written in 1886, *The Strange Case of Dr. Jekyll and Mr. Hyde.* You will recall that Dr. Jekyll is a respectable citizen who leads a double life—hiding from public view the sordid side of himself that secretly indulges in certain pleasures. We hear about this all the time. We hear about respectable citizens, people ranking in society, prominent members of our towns and cities, and by and by, their hidden life comes to light.

In this case, Dr. Jekyll is able to concoct a potion that turns him into the embodiment of his evil self. Of course, he has this potion because he has a desire to live through his evil self some of the time. He has that desire as long as he can control and be in control of the evil self. And doesn't that happen to all of us? We know we have a bad habit but we believe that we have it under control. "I don't really have the coffee habit," right? "I am not really addicted to sugar," "I can take or leave pot any time," and so forth. So we play this little balancing game. But it's a two-edged sword.

At first, Dr. Jekyll is able to safely transform himself from Dr. Jekyll to Mr. Hyde and back again. But as he indulges Mr. Hyde to a greater and greater degree, Mr. Hyde gets the upper hand. As we indulge the dweller-on-the-threshold, we give him more power and a little more power and a little more power. And of course, he hides that power. We never really know how powerful that dweller is. So we allow ourselves to believe that we are always in control.

The following excerpts are from the confession that Dr. Jekyll wrote just before he turned into Hyde and committed suicide:

> The evil side of my nature, to which I had now transferred the stamping efficacy, was less robust and less developed than the good which I had just deposed. Again, in the course of my life, which had been, after all, nine tenths a life of effort, virtue and control, it had been much less exercised and much less exhausted. And hence, as I think, it came about that Edward Hyde was so much smaller, slighter and younger than Henry Jekyll. Even as good shone upon the countenance of the one, evil was written broadly and plainly on the face of the other. . . .

> The pleasures which I had made haste to seek in my disguise were, as I have said, undignified; I would scarce use a harder term. But in the hands of Edward Hyde, they soon began to turn toward the monstrous. When I would come back from these excursions, I was often plunged into a kind of wonder at my vicarious

depravity. This familiar that I called out of my own soul, and sent forth alone to do his good pleasure, was a being inherently malign and villainous; his every act and thought centered on self; drinking pleasure with bestial avidity from any degree of torture to another; relentless like a man of stone. Henry Jekyll stood at times aghast before the acts of Edward Hyde; but the situation was apart from ordinary laws, and insidiously relaxed the grasp of conscience. It was Hyde, after all, and Hyde alone, that was guilty. Jekyll was no worse; he woke again to his good qualities seemingly un-impaired; he would even make haste, where it was possible, to undo the evil done by Hyde. And thus his conscience slumbered. . . .

Some two months before the murder of Sir Danvers, I had been out for one of my adventures, had returned at a late hour, and woke the next day in bed with somewhat odd sensations. It was in vain I looked about me; in vain I saw the decent furniture and tall proportions of my room in the square; in vain that I recognized the pattern of the bed curtains and the design of the mahogany frame; something still kept insisting that I was not where I was, that I had not wakened where I seemed to be, but in the little room in Soho where I was accustomed to sleep in the body of Edward Hyde. I smiled to myself, and, in my psychol-ogical way, began lazily to inquire into the elements of this illusion, occasionally, even as I did so, dropping back into a comfortable morning doze. I was still so engaged when, in one of my more wakeful moments, my eyes fell upon my hand. Now the hand of Henry Jekyll (as you have often remarked) was professional in shape and size: it was large, firm, white and comely. But the hand which I now saw, clearly enough, in the yellow light of a mid-London morning, lying half shut on the bedclothes, was lean, corded, knuckly, of a dusky pallor and thickly shaded with a swart growth of hair. It was the hand of Edward Hyde.

I must have stared upon it for nearly half a minute, sunk as I was in the mere stupidity of wonder, before terror woke up in my breast as sudden and startling as the crash of cymbals; and bounding from my bed, I rushed to the mirror. At the sight that met my eyes, my blood was changed into something exquisitely thin and icy. Yes, I had gone to bed Henry Jekyll, I had awakened Edward Hyde. How was this to be explained? I asked myself; and then, with another bound of terror—how was it to be remedied?...

This inexplicable incident, this reversal of my previous experience, seemed, like the Babylonian finger on the wall, to be spelling out the letters of my judgment*; and I began to reflect more seriously than ever before on the issues and possibilities of my double existence. That part of me which I had the power of projecting, had lately been much exercised and nourished; it had seemed to me of late as though the body of Edward Hyde had grown in stature, as though (when I wore that form) I were conscious of a more generous tide of blood; and I began to spy a danger that, if this were much prolonged, the balance of my nature might

---

* The Book of Daniel records the finger writing on the wall of the palace of Belshazzar, king of Babylon, "MENE, MENE, TEKEL UPARSHIN, which Daniel interpreted as meaning "God hath numbered thy kingdom, and finished it. Thou art weighed in the balances, and art found wanting. Thy kingdom is divided, and given to the Medes and Persians." [Dan. 5:26–28.]

be permanently overthrown, the power of voluntary change be forfeited, and the character of Edward Hyde become irrevocably mine....

I was slowly losing hold of my original and better self, and becoming slowly incorporated with my second and worse.

Between these two, I now felt I had to choose....

For two months, Dr. Jekyll resisted the temptation to drink his compound. But then, he writes:

I began to be tortured with throes and longings, as of Hyde struggling after freedom; and at last, in an hour of moral weakness, I once again compounded and swallowed the transforming draught....

My devil had been long caged, he came out roaring. I was conscious, even when I took the draught, of a more unbridled and more furious propensity to ill....

Again Dr. Jekyll says he began to lose control. He writes:

At all hours of the day and night, I would be taken with the premonitory shudder; above all, if I slept, or even dozed for a moment in my chair, it was always as Hyde that I awakened.... The powers of Hyde seemed to have grown with the sickliness of Jekyll.[3]

The soul in her power is reduced. She has given her light to the counterfeiting image.

Challenging the Dweller

We understand that everything that is pure and true and lovely and holy can be destroyed by the dweller-on-the-threshold. We also understand that the soul who is vulnerable, without defense, without a spiritual path is not able to defend herself against the monster of the dweller-on-the-threshold.

Sometimes when we live with the insane or those addicted to drugs or alcohol, we see that that is the potion that brings out the dark side, the violent side. And many have suffered from not realizing that this violent inner nature, when that individual turns inside out, can be seen there because the individual has not made a choice to embody the Christ and, therefore, has lost control through a drug habit or whatever may come upon him as foul spirits from without, thus triggering the actual behavior of that dweller.

The dweller is unleashed in society through the violent ones, whether they are terrorists or rapists or murderers. This is an example where the individual has not resisted the dark side of his nature, has allowed it to grow like a neglected garden where the weeds have grown and there has been no ax of John the Baptist to go to the root of that evil.

The reason that we need a master to sponsor our discipleship on the Path is that the moment we embrace the Master Jesus Christ as our Lord, we have to prove that filialty, that discipleship, by denying the dweller. And the moment we determine to challenge the dweller, we need Jesus' help. And he knows that. He comes to help us. He sends his angels. And when the soul plights her troth with the forces of light, the entire Spirit of the Great White Brotherhood, she can stand fearless before that monster within and without because she knows she stands as a part of that total Community of the Holy Spirit, that Great White Brotherhood who, because she had made her vow to defeat the dweller, will always send God's angels to her side to defeat the fallen self.

Unless we say, "Yea, Lord, I will to enter this path of discipleship. I will keep the flame of God's life in my temple because I know that ultimately that life will devour the force of anti-life," until there is a commitment and a sealing of oneself on a course, there cannot be the corresponding commitment of the hosts of the Lord to defend us against our self-created enemy.

This is why we take vows, because a vow receives the strength of God. And we keep the vow. But if we reserve the right of free will to every day decide, "Shall I be Mr. Hyde today or shall I be Dr. Jekyll?"; if we decide that we can be one self one day and one self the other, and say, "I am all right. Nothing can touch me. I am in control. I can indulge in this and that and I will come out all right"; if we are our own man, our own woman and our own boss—when we get in the stranglehold of the fallen one, we do not have an advocate before the Father.

So rather than get in that position, we go back to the mediocrity of the human consciousness. We don't go to the extreme of light and we don't go to the extremes of darkness. We are law-abiding citizens. We are good people. We do the things people do. We sit in front of the TV set. We while away our time. We look for entertainment. And we keep a pretty good ledger of good works, always banking that on one side to be our recourse in time of trouble.

But by and by that unchallenged dweller, that dweller that we have denied, lays claim to us. It says, "You have left me chained in the basement as the monster. But I will not forever be chained." And therefore, ultimately it comes out in the body as old age, disease and death or accident. There are no accidents. Accidents are when that dweller and that monster get violent and we can't handle it, and so we are impacted by that violence from without.

Star Wars

Yet another encounter with the dweller-on-the-threshold is to be found in what has become a modern-day American classic—the *Star Wars* trilogy. The hero, young Luke Skywalker, is a freedom fighter against the evil Empire. His greatest enemy is Darth Vader, who is second-in-command under the evil emperor. Darth Vader is a tall, massive figure, dressed in black, with a black helmet always covering his head—always covering his chakras.

Luke's goal is to become a Jedi knight, which requires a certain mastery of "the Force." He is instructed by Obiwan Kenobe (his teacher from higher realms) to journey to the Degoba system where he will find Yoda, the only living instructor of Jedi knights. Yoda trains Luke and warns him of the dangers of the Dark Side of the Force.

There are very interesting lessons to be gained from these movies, as we see that the individual, determining to be the Christ as a knight and a defender of freedom, becomes the embodiment of that Christ, and therefore taking that stand, has the power to convert his father (Annakin Skywalker, who had turned to the Dark Side and thus become Darth Vader) back to the path of light. The father then sees that he has been the slave of the dweller, of the head of the Evil Empire.

However, what is a bit simplistic about the ending is that that moment of truth upon death gives the individual the opportunity to reincarnate and to begin the path of slaying the not-self. The not-self is not slain in a moment's realization. That moment is a moment of conversion. Therefore, we should see the father not suddenly becoming all good and all light (as is shown in the film), but coming to the place where he will reincarnate and be accountable for all evil that he has sown. But because he takes his vow to serve the light side, he will be reinforced by the Great White Brotherhood, and he will be able to retrace his steps and slay every act of that dweller as he follows that path of his evil sowings all the way back to the point of origin and comes to the moment likewise of slaying the dweller himself.

I think the oversimplistic resolution of this series of films leaves our generation with the idea that somehow evil is a part of the sacredness of the whole experience and that the dweller is sacred and that just the realization of the unreality of evil will make it go away. We see in the scene of the final confrontation between Luke and Darth Vader that Luke says, "I will not fight." But when pushed to defend what is dearest to him, Luke will fight. And we have to understand that our nation and our land is being lusted after by those who have concluded that they can survive a nuclear war and that they will pay the price to defeat us.

If we have a nation of pacifists who say, "I will not fight," we have to find in them what it is that they will love so much that they are willing to fight for it. Will they fight for their souls? Will they fight that dweller, that planetary dweller, of the International Capitalist/Communist Conspiracy because they love their soul and other souls? If they don't love their soul, will they love the cause of freedom? Will they love Saint Germain or Jesus Christ? There has to be something so great in one's life that freedom and life itself are worth defending.

So we come to an age where self-worth is not at a high premium. And we find those who are willing to die rather than to take a stand for life, to abort life rather than to defend life.

Opportunity and Judgment

Those who take the left-handed path and do not repent of their deeds and continue to embody evil until the final day of opportunity, of them it is written in the Book of Revelation. In Revelation 20 we read:

And I saw a great white throne, and him that sat

upon it, from whose face the earth and the heaven fled away; and there was found no place for them.

And I saw the dead, small and great, stand before God; and the books were opened: and another book was opened, which is the book of life: and the dead were judged out of those things which were written in the books, according to their works.

The term "works" means karma—according to their karma.

And the sea [the astral plane] gave up the dead which were in it; and death and hell delivered up the dead which were in them: and they were judged every man according to their works [according to the causes they have set in motion by their deeds].

And death and hell were cast into the lake of fire. This is the second death.

This means that those who have fully embodied the consciousness of Death and Hell are cast into the lake of fire, and ultimately that entire plane of Death and Hell; they and their deeds are consumed by the all-consuming flame.

And whosoever was not found written in the book of life was cast into the lake of fire.

Those who are not written in the Book of Life are those who have not the threefold flame. They are the Frankenstein monsters, the godless creation, the mechanization man. They are the not-self outplayed to its ultimate self-destruction.

He that overcometh [the dweller-on-the-threshold, the counterfeiting spirit] shall inherit all things [all of God, all of Christ, all of heaven, all of the causal body]; and I will be his God, and he shall be my son.[4]

When the dweller is vanquished, there is no longer any barrier to God dwelling fully in you and you dwelling fully in God. This is the meaning of the ascension. The fire of the I AM Presence becomes our natural habitation.

> But the fearful, and unbelieving, and the abominable, and murderers, and whoremongers, and sorcerers, and idolaters, and all liars, shall have their part in the lake which burneth with fire and brimstone: which is the second death.[5]

The second death, then, is the canceling out by sacred fire of the soul that has fully identified with the dark side and through millions of years has never repented. Therefore, there is no God in him. Therefore, there is nothing to sustain any further existence. It is the mercy of the Law.

The victory of *Star Wars* is that in the hand of the Jedi knight, of the Christed one, Light cancels out Darkness. Darkness is not greater than Light, because Darkness is the inversion of Light. In reality we, the knight, are the one who has given our light that the Darth Vaders or the evil emperors may create the darkness and their legions of darkness. Therefore, the raising of the sword of light with Archangel Michael and his legions is to reclaim the light from the not-self, or the force of anti-light, to which we have once given it. This we must do because we, therefore, have been the instrument of its creation, hence its creator.

The apostle John wrote the conclusion of this mystery. He said:

> Love not the world, neither the things that are in the world. If any man love the world, the love of the Father is not in him. For all that is in the world, the lust of the flesh, and the lust of the eyes, and the pride of

life, is not of the Father, but is of the world. And the world passeth away, and the lust thereof: but he that doeth the will of God abideth for ever. Little children, it is the last time: and as ye have heard that antichrist shall come, even now are there many antichrists; whereby we know that it is the last time.[6]

The meaning of the "last time" is that we have come to the harvest; the path of our soul and her Christhood is fully ripened and before us. The path of the dweller has come to its ultimate conclusion. For us individually, we know that this is an hour when we are called to ascend to God.

It is as though it were the last opportunity and the final initiation. And it *is*, for our civilization and our planet, not the end of the world but simply the end of an epoch, an end of a long, long period of tens of thousands of years and longer, when we have been moving toward this moment of the ultimate and supreme choice.

Jesus has reminded us of the necessity of facing the fact that there is embodied evil on this planet and that the force of planetary evil, as well as our own carnal mind, must be slain. Remember, when we say embodied evil, we mean those individuals who, having free will, have chosen to embody the Darkness rather than the Light, the monster of the human creation, the dweller-on-the-threshold, in the place of their Holy Christ Self. Jesus said:

> When you look at planetary evil, when you look into the very teeth of the Watchers [the fallen angels] and the serpents who parade before you daily on the television screen, you must surely come to the place of the mature son of God who must say: "In my heart I know what I must do in order to rid the planet of the Evil One. I know that I must conquer where I am and

not delay and not tarry! I know that I must overcome in God! I know that He awaits my coming, that He might speak the word through me of judgment that will be finis—the end!—the final end of the doctrines of the wicked."

Beloved hearts, if you would know the Truth, I would tell you that evil still stalks the world so that the good people who desire to follow me will have a perpetual and inescapable reminder that they have not yet slain their own carnal mind! And they have contented themselves to remain at the halfway point, satisfied to feed the beast and thereby tame it rather than starve it and slay it. Many have made the choice to feed the beast, satisfy it with creature comforts and various addictions of the various chakras. But, beloved, choose not the way of all flesh—and know that your victory is an individual and planetary victory and that the planetary dweller-on-the-threshold is reduced by the power and the magnitude of your overcoming of the energy veil within yourself. And ultimately everyone upon earth, if he would ascend, must slay the enemy within and the world consciousness of sin.

AN ENCOUNTER WITH THE DWELLER

Among the early portrayals in literature of the dweller-on-the-threshold is one from Brother of the Third Degree, *by Will Garver, first published in 1894. In this classic of esoteric fiction, Garver paints a vivid image of the dweller and of the soul who must, in a final encounter before passing on to higher initiations, consign the remnant of that dweller into the sacred fire.*

As though seized by an insane idea, and despite the oppressive heat, I built a blazing fire upon the hearth, and sitting down before it gazed into its red flames. As I did so the licking flames grew higher, and leaping up seemed to lean forward toward me; then I became as though entranced and lost the power of motion. At the same moment the horrible creature I had seen at the Durant mansion formed in the flames before me; but this time instead of repelling, it seemed to fascinate, and as I leaned forward I recognized its evil and malignant features as my own. It smiled hideously, and continuing to look, it became attractive. As I did not repel, it came toward me; but now, my God! What is it? It shapes into a living skeleton, and its bony form, covered with dry and wrinkled flesh, shone with a greasy gloss of reddish-green. It extended its bony hands to embrace me, I felt them on my neck and shoulders, I inhaled its sickening, poisonous breath; then, as its bony fingers clasped me around the neck as though to choke me, a faint ray of light dawned upon my mind, and I uttered the one word—"Iole!"

An awful, demoniacal shriek rang in my ears; a groan of despair, and the form was sucked back toward the fire. It struggled and pulled toward me, its fiery eyes looking from their sunken depths with a wild, satanic glare; but a white form now stood before me, and with outstretched hand pushed the monster into the flames. With one last wild shriek, it fell into the fire, and as though made of pitch was consumed by the lurid flames. At the same moment, as by an instantaneous change, my soul was filled with light, and looking up I beheld the radiant form of my glorious sister.

"Iole, my savior!" I cried.

"Only the Iole in thyself can be thy savior; only the Christ, Krishna, God or Master within can save thee," answered her mind to mine.

"Thou hast just now slain the last shadow of thy demon nature formed in lives gone by; and now thou art absolutely pure. All men must meet and slay their demon before they pass on [to higher initiations], for this demon shadow ever awaits them at the threshold, and unless they conquer they cannot pass through. When you called for me you called upon your God, for I am but a symbol of the God within your soul."

CHAPTER FIVE

The Lost Teachings of Jesus on the Enemy Within

Elizabeth Clare Prophet

Paul spoke on the enemy within to the Romans. He revealed his soul's intimate facing of the living Christ and the Adversary. He was not ashamed to tell us of his struggle between light and darkness.

> For we know that the law is spiritual: but I am carnal, sold under sin [karma]. For that which I do I allow not: for what I would do, that do I not; but what I hate, that do I. If then I do that which I would not, I consent unto the law that it is good.
>
> Now then it is no more I that do it, but sin that dwelleth in me. For I know that in me (that is, in my flesh,) dwelleth no good thing: for to will is present with me; but how to perform that which is good I find not. For the good that I would I do not: but the evil which I would not, that I do.
>
> Now if I do that I would not, it is no more I that do it, but sin that dwelleth in me. I find then a law, that, when I would do good, evil is present with me.

For I delight in the law of God after the inward man [the Holy Christ Self]: but I see another law in my members, warring against the law of my mind, and bringing me into captivity to the law of sin which is in my members.

O wretched man that I am! who shall deliver me from this body of death?

I thank God through Jesus Christ our Lord. So then with the mind I myself serve the law of God; but with the flesh the law of sin.[1]

We see the enemy without. To conquer that enemy, we must conquer the enemy within. We must obey the command "Know thyself and know thine enemy."

This has always been the conundrum facing those who would be disciples of Christ Jesus. The solving of this problem of being has never been more important than it is today, when this saving of the planet demands that we put on the full mantle of our Christhood. Paul wrote, "that ye put off concerning the former conversation the old man, which is corrupt according to the deceitful lusts; and be renewed in the spirit of your mind; and that ye put on the new man, which after God is created in righteousness and true holiness." "For to be carnally minded is death; but to be spiritually minded is life and peace."[2]

Jesus has called us to enter into a new and very personal master-disciple relationship with him. He has said:

Discipleship in this age is the call of the Cosmic Christ.... I call you to be now the embodiment of all that I AM and to receive me that you might have with me henceforth the most direct relationship. I call for a purpose, and it is the step-by-step containment of the light. I call you to my fold not in the general sense but in the specific sense of knowing that a teaching, a way of life, a Spirit of the Resurrection cannot endure upon earth unless, truly, ten thousand determine in this hour of my appearing to embody the fullness of myself....

I am come ready to place upon you a crown of everlasting life when you shall have triumphed over the lesser nature and out of love and purest love magnetized the infilling of the Word, of the Holy Ghost, of the water of Life and the Blood that is my Being, my Self.[3]

And so we say to Jesus in response, "Yea, Lord, come into my temple and abide with me forever." In Minneapolis, on November 1, All Saints' Day, Jesus said:

Blessed hearts, it is the hour and this is the day of the marking of the hour, November 1, 1987. Mark it well, beloved, for it is a date written in the Book of Life.... I have come to bring you, then, the Word of our Father, and it is this: The hour has come for you to understand that nothing less than becoming the Christ will suffice as fulfillment or requirement of the Law.... This is the day that the path of thy Christhood must begin in earnest. Not postponed till tomorrow but today: my Christ, thy Christ, one.

Counting this day as the first day, if you will, of an earnest discipleship unto my flame and heart, I draw you if you will be drawn. I receive you if you will indeed be received. Therefore, beloved, know that I, Jesus, declare this day, formally with my Father, as the commencement of a path for lightbearers of the world who know that in my mantle and in my momentum there is a gift to be received—to be earned and won.... I AM your Jesus. Now I say to you, Be my Christ![4]

If we would answer this calling of our Lord and make our election sure to be his disciples, we must answer the same question that Paul asked: Who shall deliver me from this body of death—this warring in my members?

When we look to find the lost teachings of Jesus on this subject that is squarely before each one of us, not only as we desire to be living disciples with Jesus but as we desire to unite with him in the resurrection, in the life everlasting, we must turn again to the Christian Gnostics of the first centuries after the birth of Christ. They have left us a revealing legacy of teaching on this subject. It is at once mystical and practical.

The Gnostic Tradition

Gnosticism was a movement within early Christianity that flourished during the second century at a time when doctrines and organizational structure of the Church as we know it today were not yet solidified. Gnostic writings have provided insight, therefore, into some of the controversies that existed in the formative years of Christianity—controversies that centered around the crucial questions of what Jesus did and did not teach, what he did and did not intend his church to be like.

Gnosticism was actually a movement composed of a diverse group of sects with varied beliefs and lifestyles— ranging from a strict asceticism to a libertine outlook on life. As prominent Gnostic scholar Hans Jonas has pointed out, "the movement itself transcended ethnic and denominational boundaries."[5]

What they did have in common, to a greater or lesser degree, was that they did not accept the Church's newly developed creeds, doctrines and hierarchical structure. The Gnostics did not agree with the early Church Fathers and ecclesiastics who had vested the sole authority for teaching and preaching in the hands of the clerics. And they did not accept the Church's strict criteria for deciding what was and was not to be labeled "scripture."

The Gnostics themselves claimed to be the guardians of the mystery teaching handed down through certain of Jesus' disciples. These teachings, they said, had been given by Jesus to an inner circle of initiates during his Palestine ministry, during the period between his resurrection and ascension, or after his ascension as new revelation.

The Gnostics did not believe that at Jesus' ascension, the door of access to the Word of the Lord was shut forever. They did not believe that on the occasion of his ascent, the scripture was finalized. They believed that they could experience for themselves an intimate communion with Jesus, that he could impart to them individually new insights and teachings, very personal, spoken in the secret chamber of the heart through that very same Christ Presence that he was.

The writings of the Gnostics that embodied these revelations are not among the accepted scriptures of Christianity that have come down to us today. Most of their works have not survived. Why is this so? Because the early Church Fathers, threatened by the popularity of a teaching that challenged the orthodox position, condemned the Gnostics and banned their works.

What they were condemning was freedom of religion and the spirit of liberty we receive by Christ that sets the captive soul free. They were denying freedom to pursue the quest. They were denying the freedom of the soul's intimate, personal and individual relationship with Jesus Christ, with the archangels and with the saints in heaven. Thus, orthodoxy becomes the denial of individual spiritual freedom, both in the first centuries following Jesus and today.

As a result of this banning of the works of the Gnostics, almost all of their writings were destroyed. Until the last century, all we really knew about the Gnostics came from their greatest enemies, the Church Fathers, who wrote scathing and lengthy denunciations of their ideological foes.

Therefore, it wasn't until the translation of two original Gnostic documents in the late nineteenth century, Codex Askewianus (Pistis Sophia) and Codex Brucianus, then the astounding discovery in 1945 of fifty-two ancient Gnostic texts at Nag Hammadi, Egypt, that some of the lost teachings of the Gnostics came fully to light and the Gnostics could finally speak for themselves.

The word *Gnosticism* is derived from the Greek word *gnosis,* which means knowledge or understanding. To the Gnostics, knowledge was the key to salvation and ignorance one's greatest enemy. Gnosis was a knowledge of one's self against the backdrop of one's understanding of God, of the universe, and of good and evil.

The Church Fathers severely criticized the Gnostics for delving into these matters. And the clergy today have equal condemnation for the same movement that is rising up as the New Age movement that discovers the Reality of God within.

Church Father Tertullian, in his treatise "On Prescription Against Heretics," which was written about 196 A.D., complains, "The same subject-matter is discussed over and over again..., the same arguments are involved: Whence comes evil? Why is it permitted? What is the origin of man? and in what way does he come?... Whence comes God?"

Tertullian adds that the true Christian wants "no curious disputation after possessing Christ Jesus, no inquiring after enjoying the gospel! With our faith, we desire no further belief."[6]

He complains against the very quest of the soul, the

questioning that allows us to arrive at the source of the answer. The very process of questioning, when it is sincere and profound, when it is directed to the living Jesus Christ, brings him to our heart. And he has never failed to answer our questions or our needs when we have asked him. What Tertullian is denying is a scientific statement of Being and of Truth. Not only is this denial of spiritual inquiry but of a scientific understanding of man in his relationship to God.

For the Gnostics who would not be deterred by this condemnation, there was no salvation without the quest. For them, Jesus was the messenger and guide sent from higher realms to set the highest example and teach the mysteries that would lead the disciple to a realization of gnosis. But they believed that each individual was responsible for his own salvation. The apostle Paul also says this (and this is in our canon): "Work out your own salvation with fear and trembling,"[7] which means with awe before the majesty of God and with an equal awe before the unreality of the not-self.

A Goal of Personal Christhood

The goal of the Gnostics was nothing short of personal Christhood, the realization within of all that was in Christ Jesus. *Christ* comes from the Greek *Christos,* meaning the "anointed one." They sought the same anointing that was received by the son of man, the anointing of the light of the Son of God.

The Gnostic Gospel of Philip, named for that apostle and probably written in the second half of the third century in Syria, calls the one who has achieved gnosis "no longer a Christian but a Christ"—one anointed of the light of the I AM Presence. "You saw the Spirit, you became spirit. You saw Christ, you became Christ. You saw the Father, you shall become Father.... What you see you shall become."[8]

When we understand the mystery of the Old Testament teaching "no man can see God and live,"[9] we will see that this teaching of Philip is the same. Jesus tells us that the true meaning of that statement is, "No man can see God and live any longer as man. He must live thereafter as God." Therefore, the seeing is the taking unto oneself of that eternal life.

The Gospel of Thomas contains many statements along the same vein. It was translated from an original Greek manuscript, which scholars believe may have been written as early as the second half of the first century. Scholar Helmut Koester writes:

> According to the *Gospel of Thomas,* the basic religious experience is not only the recognition of one's divine identity, but more specifically the recognition of one's origin (the light) and destiny (the repose). In order to return to one's origin, the disciple is to become separate from the world by "stripping off" the fleshly garment and "passing by" the present corruptible existence; then the disciple can experience the new world, the kingdom of light, peace, and life.[10]

In its opening paragraphs, the Gospel of Thomas also describes a certain process of soul-searching and striving that will face the disciple who is uncomfortable with his present level on the path of discipleship.

I think we are unanimous that each and every one of us faces those moments of uncomfortability with the present level of our discipleship. For we have enough of light and Christ in us to see the inadequacy of the lesser self. We have enough light in us to see the great beauty of the Lord Jesus Christ and to know that we have a walk to walk to be fully like him. The subject of the enemy within is based on this very focus, the uncomfortability in this discipleship.

The Gospel of Thomas begins:

> These are the secret sayings which the living Jesus spoke and which Didymos Judas Thomas wrote down.
> And he said, "Whoever finds the interpretation of these sayings will not experience death."

This death is the death of the soul; in other words, this person will not experience the limitation of the body of mortality, though that one may yet pass through the normal process of transition.

> Jesus said, "Let him who seeks continue seeking until he finds. When he finds, he will become troubled. When he becomes troubled, he will be astonished, and he will rule over the All....
> "The Kingdom is inside of you, and it is outside of you. When you come to know yourselves, then you will become known, and you will realize that it is you who are the sons of the living Father. But if you will not know yourselves, you dwell in poverty and it is you who are that poverty."...
> Jesus said, "Recognize what is in your sight, and that which is hidden from you will become plain to you. For there is nothing hidden which will not become manifest."[11]

The Teaching of Silvanus, a tractate discovered at Nag Hammadi, makes the point that the disciple needs to look within to find the answers:

> Knock on yourself as upon a door, and walk upon yourself as on a straight road. For if you walk on the road, it is impossible for you to go astray. And if you

knock with this one (Wisdom), you knock on hidden treasuries.[12]

Knocking on the door of the Real Self who is Christ, we have access to the treasury of wisdom that is stored in the Great Causal Body.

The Real Self and the Not-Self

When we study the writings of the Gnostics, we find that the emphasis on gnosis was a two-edged sword: gnosis was not only knowledge of the Real Self—the Christ Self that one was in the process of becoming—but it was also the knowledge of the lower self, the karmic self, including the "not self" or "anti-self"—"this body of death," which Paul lamented.

The Gospel of Thomas is explicit on this point:

> "If you bring forth what is within you, what you bring forth will save you. If you do not bring forth what is within you, what you do not bring forth will destroy you."[13]

In the Gospel of Thomas, Jesus is quoted as saying to Salome:

> "I am He who exists from the Undivided. I was given some of the things of my father."
>
> Salome said, "I am your disciple."
>
> Jesus said to her, "Therefore I say, if he is undivided, he will be filled with light, but if he is divided, he will be filled with darkness."[14]

The same teaching is given to us that we cannot serve God and mammon. The house divided against itself cannot stand.[15]

The Gospel of Philip explains that the process of rooting out the destructive element within that would, if it could, remain unseen and undealt with is very necessary to the path toward union.

> So long as the root of wickedness is hidden, it is strong. But when it is recognized it is dissolved. When it is revealed it perishes. That is why the word says, "Already the ax is laid at the root of the trees." It will not merely cut—what is cut sprouts again—but the ax penetrates deeply until it brings up the root. Jesus pulled out the root of the whole place, while others did it only partially. As for ourselves, let each one of us dig down after the root of evil which is within one, and let one pluck it out of one's heart from the root. It will be plucked out if we recognize it.[16]

We must see it in order to render it powerless.

The Counterfeiting Spirit

Other Gnostic texts examine in great detail this "root of wickedness," its origin and its defeat. They speak of a "counterfeit" or "counterfeiting spirit" (which has also been translated as "antagonistic" or "despicable spirit") that seeks to lead mankind astray "so that he will not know his perfection."[17]

The most intricate teaching of this subject comes from the third-century Gnostic text Pistis Sophia. This book includes a series of dialogues between Jesus and his disciples. In these dialogues, Jesus reveals to them the higher mysteries.

In one section, he explains that there are two elements given to the soul who is to reincarnate: the power and the counterfeiting spirit. The counterfeiting spirit is created by "the rulers of the great Fate."

We can see the rulers as being the fallen angels who move men and nations by their karma—karma being an equivalent word to fate. Our fate is our karma and our karma is our fate. And therefore, we have seen that the false hierarchies of Antichrist do seek to move to ensnare us through our own karma.

The counterfeiting spirit is created by "the rulers of the great Fate" who

> "...give the old soul a cup of forgetfulness out of the seed of wickedness, filled with all the different desires and all forgetfulness. And straightway, when that soul shall drink out of the cup, it forgetteth all the regions to which it hath gone, and all the chastisements in which it hath travelled. And that cup of the water of forgetfulness becometh body outside the soul, and it resembleth the soul in all its figures and maketh itself like it, which is what is called the counterfeiting spirit....
>
> "[The counterfeiting spirit] bideth outside the soul, being a vesture for it and resembling it in every way."[18]

The forgetfulness that is upon us we know well. We enter this life, and just prior to taking on that newly formed body, we are fully aware of the heaven-world and beings of light, our spiritual guides, the masters, the Lords of Karma and loved ones. For a while in that tiny body we remember. But very quickly the veil of forgetfulness comes upon us.

We forget in our waking state our inner experiences in the spiritual octaves of light. Our forgetfulness from hour to hour and day to day is of the very teaching we espouse. We forget we have an I AM Presence and a Holy Christ Self. We think we don't forget; but when we cry out in fear and despair and see the darkness of the world, why, of course, we are forgetting. If we did not forget and if we did remember, we would be in the full glory of that I AM Presence moment by moment. Thus, forgetfulness is a curse of mortality, whatever its source.

The "power," on the other hand, is inbreathed "within into that soul" to "give sense unto the soul, in order that it may seek after the works of the Light of the Height always. And that power is like the species of the soul in every form and resembleth it. . . . And the portion of that power remaineth within the soul, so that the soul can stand."[19]

We see, then, that there are three elements that figure at our birth—the soul, the power and the counterfeit spirit.

When Mary Magdalene asks Jesus the question, "Who constraineth the man until he sinneth," the Master delivers a discourse on the counterfeiting spirit.

"When the babe is born, the power is feeble in it, and the soul is feeble in it, and also the counterfeiting spirit is feeble in it; in a word, the three together are feeble, without any one of them sensing anything, whether good or evil, because of the load of forgetfulness which is very heavy. . . .

"And little by little the power and the soul and the counterfeiting spirit grow, and every one of them senseth according to its nature: the power senseth to seek after the light of the height; the soul on the other hand senseth to seek after the region of righteousness which is mixed, which is the region of the commixture; the counterfeiting spirit on the other hand seeketh after all evils and lusts and all sins. . . .

"And after this the counterfeiting spirit contriveth and senseth all sins and the evil which the rulers of the great Fate have commanded for the soul, and it maketh them for the soul.

"And the inner power stirreth the soul to seek after the region of Light and the whole godhead; and the

counterfeiting spirit leadeth away the soul and compelleth it continually to do all its lawless deeds, all its
mischiefs and all its sin, and is persistently allotted to
the soul and is hostile to it, and making it to do all this
evil and all these sins.

"And it goadeth on the retributive servitors, so that
they are witnesses in all the sins which it will make it
do. Moreover also if it will rest in the night or by day,
it stirreth it in dreams or in lusts of the world, and
maketh it to lust after all the things of the world. In a
word, it driveth it into all the things which the rulers
have commanded for it and it is hostile to the soul,
making it do what pleaseth it not.

"Now, therefore, Mary, this is in fact the foe of the
soul, and this compelleth it until it doeth all sins."...

"When, therefore, the time of the chastisements of
that soul in the judgments of the rulers of the midst
shall be completed, the counterfeiting spirit leadeth the
soul up out of all the regions of the rulers of the midst
and bringeth it before the light of the sun according to
the commandment of the First Man, Yew, and bringeth
it before the judge, the Virgin of Light. And she proveth
that soul and findeth that it is a sinning soul, and
casteth her light-power into it for its standing-upright
and because of the body and the community of sense,—
the type of which I will tell you at the expansion of the
universe. And the Virgin Light sealeth that soul and
handeth it over to one of her receivers and will have it
cast into a body which is suitable to the sins which it
hath committed."[20]

We see, then, that there are those elements of those
powers and rulers who are of the fallen ones who delight in

bringing the soul before trial and before the courts of the world and the courts of hell. We see that the virgin light is the defender of the soul. But the virgin light must also assess how the soul has chosen between the counterfeiting spirit and the Universal Light. And therefore, the conclusion of the judgment is according to one's creation. The body that one will wear, the plane on which one will serve will be the fruit of this passing through the experience of the two-edged sword dividing the Real Self and the not-self.

Jesus continued again in the discourse and said: "If on the contrary it is a soul which hath not hearkened unto the counterfeiting spirit in all its works, but hath become good [God] and hath received the mysteries of the Light, ... it uttereth the mystery of the undoing of the seals and all the bonds of the counterfeiting spirit with which the rulers have bound it to the soul. . . ."[21]

At that moment, then, the soul, having chosen the Good, does release and is released from this counterfeiting spirit, this dweller on the threshold.

"And in that moment it becometh a great light-stream, shining exceedingly, and the retributive receivers who have led it forth out of the body, are afraid of the light of that soul and fall on their faces. And in that moment that soul becometh a great light-stream, it becometh entirely wings of light, and penetrateth all the regions of the rulers [the fallen ones] and all of the orders of the Light, until it reacheth the region of its kingdom up to which it hath received mysteries. . . ."[22]

Forgiveness through the Violet Flame

And Mary ... said: "My Lord, in what type then do the baptisms forgive sins?..."

Jesus answered,

"Now, therefore, he who shall receive the mysteries of the baptisms, then the mystery of them becometh a great, exceedingly violent, wise fire and it burneth up the sins and entereth into the soul secretly and consumeth all the sins which the counterfeiting spirit hath made fast on to it."[23]

Here is the prophecy of the sacred fire, the all-consuming fire of God, given to us portion by portion as the violet flame. The violet flame is a stepped-down version of the sacred fire; for the sacred fire itself, before that soul is transfigured and sealed in her wedding garment, would utterly annihilate the soul. And therefore, the fire of this baptism of forgiveness is the violet flame that creeps secretly into the chamber and sanctuary of the soul to consume the cause, effect, record of sin.

"And when it hath finished purifying all the sins which the counterfeiting spirit hath made fast on to the soul, it entereth into the body secretly and pursueth all the pursuers secretly and separateth them off on the side of the portion of the body."[24]

And just so does the violet flame that you invoke steal into the recesses of the marrow of the bones and between the cells and in the etheric body and the astral body and all the sheaths of consciousness of the soul. The violet flame steals in and erases those sins that the retributive servitors have put upon us, leading us into the captivity of sin and the law of sin warring in the members. All this we are delivered of by our God if we come to that hour where the power and the strength in us and the soul by free will do choose to glorify God and to deny this counterfeiting spirit.

"I AM Come to Send Fire on the Earth"

One of the most enduring and endearing statements of Jesus in our own scripture is, "I am come to send fire on the earth."[25] This fire is a sacred fire unto those who have the wedding garment, and the pure power of that fire is the means of our translation in the ascension. To those yet shorn of it, yet possessed of this counterfeiting spirit, the violet flame is the great grace of the Holy Ghost. And so that fire is sent to you not alone by Jesus, your Lord, who has saved you for this victory, but by your own Holy Christ Self. If you will but make the call for the violet flame, your Holy Christ Self will shower you with violet flame daily.

And if you will combine the call with the commitment to be the disciple of Christ and the absolute God-determination to put down the counterfeiting spirit and its alliance with fallen angels and demons, you will see the victory now. "Yet in my flesh shall I see God"[26] is the fiat, the here-and-now affirmation of that living spirit of the I AM THAT I AM with us. Let us not procrastinate this encounter, this glorious victory, this overcoming. Let us awaken in the morning to rejoice that God has given to us another day to strive with that force and to enter into the light.

When the saviour had said this, he said unto his disciples: "Understand ye in what manner I discourse with you?"

Then Mary started forward and said: "Yea, my Lord, in truth I enquire closely into all the words which thou sayest.... And again thou hast distinguished it clearly, saying: 'I have a baptism, to baptize in it; and how shall I endure, how shall I endure until it is accomplished? Think ye I am come to cast peace on the earth? Nay, but I am come to cast division. For from now on five will be in one house; three will be divided against two, and two against three.' This, my Lord, is the word which thou hast spoken clearly."[27]

When Jesus says, "I came not to send peace, but a sword,"[28] he is saying, "I will not leave you in peace, dwelling in your body as a soul, the Christ on one hand and the counterfeiting spirit on the other. I will not give you peace so long as you tolerate this division within your house."

Thus, the sword is the two-edged sword. Know thy Real Self. Know thy enemy as the not-self. And choose you this day whom you will serve.

If Jesus is come to cast fire in the earth and to give us a baptism that he must delay till we are ready, shall we not call it forth and say, "Yea, Lord, baptize me this day with thy violet flame. Come into my house this day. Bind the oppressor of my soul"? Shall we not determine to conquer the enemy within that we might be free, one-pointed and wholly one, in possession of the All, to face the adversary without?

This is the message of the lost teachings of Jesus. Every day we postpone the triumph over the not-self, we are postponing our taking our stand to defend the children of the light against the world powers of the adversary in Church and State that are the oppressors of my people.

Thus we see that though we may say we desire to take a stand for Saint Germain and Jesus Christ, if we do not take a stand in our own house, our words are not true and we cannot receive the reinforcement of the seven archangels to do that work of Christ. For if God gives more power to you while you retain the counterfeiting spirit, that counterfeiting spirit will take from you that power, will take from you that light in a moment of indulgence, in a moment of descending to its level of deceit and self-deception.

Therefore, God has said as his Law, "I will not give to you more light than you are able to retain. I will not give to you any test that you cannot pass or any adversary that you cannot conquer." Therefore, level by level, we face this not-self.

The Eye of the Vortex of the Anti-Self

Another Gnostic teaching on the not-self is found in the works of Basilides, a second-century Gnostic teacher of Alexandria who claimed to possess the secret teaching of the apostle Peter. Author Jean Doresse writes:

> One of the most original portions, it seems, of the teaching of Basilides dealt with the causes of the passions and the conditions for the salvation of the soul. His doctrine upon this point was further elucidated by his son Isidore in his treatise *On the Additional Soul*. The passions, being lower, constituted as it were a second soul, which was added by the lower powers to that which man received from on high. This second soul was made up of spirits external to the former—of bestial or ferocious instincts which, producing desires in their own image, weigh man down and drag him into sin.[29]

Church Father Clement of Alexandria wrote:

> The Basilidians are accustomed to give the name of appendages [or accretions] to the passions. These essences, they say, have a certain substantial existence, and are attached to the rational soul, owing to a certain

turmoil and primitive confusion. . . . On to this nucleus other bastard and alien natures of the essence grow, such as those of the wolf, ape, lion, goat, etc. And when the peculiar qualities of such natures appear round the soul, they cause the desires of the soul to become like to the special natures of these animals, for they imitate the actions of those whose characteristics they bear.[30]

This is a teaching that we can understand in the light of what we have been told concerning the accretion of negative karma in a spiral that is called the electronic belt, which is in the shape of a kettledrum that extends beneath our feet. We understand that certain vibrations of negative karma take on an identity; they take on the vibration of certain animal forms and states of animal consciousness. Therefore, we know that in the subconscious, we can have on the astral plane these figures, animal-like, that represent our sowings less than the Christ estate.

At the eye of the vortex of this untransmuted energy in the electronic belt, which each of us does bear until we transmute 100 percent of our karma, we find that there is the consciousness of the anti-self. It is the eye of the vortex. This is the not-self that is personified. And we have called the personification of this not-self the dweller-on-the-threshold. (*Counterfeiting spirit* is a synonym for *dweller-on-the-threshold*.)

This term came down through the Theosophical movement to denote in one sense "the embodied karmic consequences or results of the man's past, haunting the thresholds which the . . . initiate must pass before he can advance or progress into a higher degree of initiation."[31] What this means is that as long as we go along in the human sense of simply being human beings and doing the things that human beings do on this planet, we will not hit the threshold of initiation.

The threshold is a higher step that we must step upon in order to go through the door of a new consciousness, a new retreat, a new initiation.

The moment the soul would go beyond the barriers that the human consciousness and human society have determined for it, she will meet the dweller-on-the-threshold, who will say, "Thus far and no farther. You cannot pass. I will not let you escape my vibration and my consciousness." Yet the soul has created this dweller in ignorance and in forgetfulness in all previous lives and in this life.

This dweller has become a sorcerer's apprentice. In order to retain its life, it must now keep the soul in slavery, because in slavery, the soul, in her moments of indulgence, selfishness and forgetfulness, will give to that dweller more energy by which that dweller can live. This miscreation of the soul has become her archenemy, preventing her from advancing on the path of initiation.

CHAPTER SIX

The Awakening of the Dweller-on-the-Threshold

Jesus the Christ

Hail, beloved of my heart! I am in the midst of the sanctuary of my own, and I abide in your heart under the shadow of the Almighty—even your mighty I AM Presence.

From the heart of the ages, from the heart of the Ancient of Days, I bring comfort and a sword. Be seated then, my own.

I come in anticipation of our celebration of the resurrection. I come beforehand to establish a pillar of that resurrection fire here upon this altar. Let no staff, then, cross this step or stand where the messenger stands until the fulfilling of the purpose of this flame on Easter Sunday.

Therefore, beloved, know that heaven—Alpha himself, the blessed Father—desires to increase day by day your assimilation of resurrection's fires. Understand, then, the meaning of the flame of the resurrection. Understand, then, the meaning of the penetration of the rainbow rays of God accelerating as a bubbling fountain, a life-giving force, an energizing force.

Understand that the resurrection flame is a flame of the awakening, awakening then that must come to the heart of each one. All that is in thee must be awakened, must be brought to the surface.[1]

Christ in You Is Awakened— The Sleeping Serpent Is Also Awakened

God has sent me with this flame this day because ye are able to bear it, because Christ in you is awakened. Truth is awakened first. And as the messengers have held the balance against the day of the awakening of the carnal mind, so you have prospered and increased in love and in your witness of Truth.

Now cometh the hour when resurrection's fires must also awaken in you that awareness of the sleeping serpent—on the one hand, the dweller-on-the-threshold, the anti-self; on the other hand, the life-force, the sacred fire out of the base-of-the-spine chakra.

These are most powerful energies. The energy of eternal life ascending in the temple is the calling of the Lord and of the Mother. It demands obedience and submission unto all of the flowers of the chakras, for the life-force makes permanent that which it contacts.

Therefore, the sleeping serpent of the dweller-on-the-threshold must first be awakened and bound in the name I AM THAT I AM by the soul who is clothed upon with her own Christ Self. With the binding, then, of this not-self and the accumulation of its works in the coil of the electronic belt,[2] there may then transpire the awakening of the sleeping serpent of the coiled Kundalini, the life-force itself.

May I remind you that this is the path of the ascended masters and of the ascension. This is not the path of the false gurus of the East who create, out of sensation and a yoga that is not lawful, a sexual activity and attempt to raise that life-force without the Holy Spirit but only by the stimulation of the chakras, stimulating the energy to rise when the attainment is not there.

You will discover, beloved hearts, that those who pursue this left-handed path then use that life-force to endow the dweller-on-the-threshold with permanence. These are the dark ones, and their seeming power is the misuse of the ascension flame to give immortality to the human ego. This, beloved ones, is the means whereby those on the left-handed path, the black magicians themselves, do gain the ability to work their works.

The Alchemical Marriage

Understanding then the mystery, all the more, little ones, ought you to run unto the Lord to be hidden in the garments of the Christ,[3] to run to the beloved Christ Self and desire above all else union with that Christ, who will bring to you chastening and outer turmoil and persecution and direct knowledge with the hatred of this world. But that Christ will not awaken in you the Kundalini until you are sealed in the alchemical marriage of the Christ of your being.

I have preached to you before concerning your striving for this marriage. May it be so among you—those who consider marriage as the next step on the Path, those who are already married in the rites accorded by God for those children evolving on earth, and those who remain unwedded in the physical sense.

Let all reconsider, then, approaching the celebration of the resurrection this Easter, that we desire to dedicate our coming together to the alchemical marriage, to the resurrection of the soul unto the Christ Self worldwide in the body of God that all might escape the wiles of the dweller-on-the-threshold of their own being until they may stand forth in Christ a knight, a lady of the flame, wielding the two-edged sword to bind that fallen one, that anti-self.

This is the desire of my heart—that you shall at least participate in this ritual on the cycling of your own cosmic clock to celebrate that union at Easter. And forty days hence, in the hour of the celebration of my ascension, you may use that day and that fire of my ascension flame to *slay!* then, the not-self and to slay the carnal mind and to get that victory over the beast[4] that it may no longer tempt and pull you away from the very threshold of the bridal chamber of your Lord.[5]

The Ritual of Slaying the Not-Self

Realize, then, that this ritual of entering in, of union, and of the slaying of the not-self is something that is repeated, even as you repeat the holy days of the year and celebrate again and again the birth of the Christ Child and each of the points of acceleration on my own path. Would to God there might be a true calendar of my life whereby you could enter in more fully to my footsteps in all of the thirty-three years.

Thus, understand that this particular ritual of Easter is most important. It is part of the divine plan of Serapis Bey that you might prepare and weave the Deathless Solar Body.

Brides of Christ are ye, fully and fairly chosen. Now you must choose so to be. You must not wait with trepidation the day of the awakening of the dweller, but run to greet that enemy. Fully clothed upon with the armour of God, you will say:

You have no power over me! You may not threaten or mar the face of my God within my soul. You may not taunt or

tempt me with past or present or future, for I AM hid with Christ in God. I AM his bride. I AM accepted by the LORD.

You have no power to destroy me! Therefore, be bound! by the LORD himself.

Your day is done! You may no longer inhabit this temple.

And then, my beloved, you wield that **mighty sword** as God wields it through you. And in the name I AM THAT I AM, so there is the binding of that foe with these words:

Be bound! you tempter of my soul. Be bound! you point of pride of the original fall of the fallen ones! You have no power, no reality, no worth. You occupy no time or space of my being.

You have no power in my temple. You may no longer steal the light of my chakras. You may not steal the light of my heart flame or my I AM Presence.

Be bound! then, O Serpent and his seed and all implants of the sinister force, for I AM THAT I AM!

I AM the Son of God this day, and I occupy this temple fully and wholly until the coming of the LORD, until the New Day, until all be fulfilled, and until this generation of the seed of Serpent pass away.

Burn through, O living Word of God!

By the power of Brahma, Vishnu and Shiva, in the name Brahman: I AM THAT I AM and I stand and I cast out the dweller.

Let him be bound by the power of the LORD's host! Let him be consigned to the flame of the sacred fire of Alpha and Omega, that that one may not go out to tempt the innocent and the babes in Christ.

Blaze the power of Elohim!

Elohim of God—Elohim of God—Elohim of God

Descend now in answer to my call. As the mandate of the LORD—as Above, so below—occupy now.

Bind the fallen self! Bind the synthetic self! Be out then!

Bind the fallen one! For there is no more remnant or residue in my life of any, or any part of that one.

Lo, I AM, in Jesus' name, the victor over Death and Hell!

Lo, I AM, in Jesus' name, the victor over Death and Hell!

Lo, I AM THAT I AM in me—in the name of Jesus Christ—is here and now the victor over Death and Hell!

Lo! it is done.

This judgment, my beloved, you may recite with me by means of the electronic recording and therefore have the power of my mantle in the binding of that one.

Jesus' Encounter with the
Planetary Dweller-on-the-Threshold

Remember, then, my fast in the wilderness.[6] The encounter with Satan was the encounter with the planetary dweller-on-the-threshold who was yet unbound until the hour of the Two Witnesses in this century.[7]

Realize this: that though he was bound and judged and had no power over me, his end could not come until other saints had also overcome his power and his abuse of that power of the Woman and the Manchild, his abuse of the power of the Kundalini fire. This is the secret of the wiles of all fallen ones. Know it well, for this knowledge will serve you in the day of your confrontation with the enemy and your victory.

Therefore, you may call for the judgment of all fallen ones who misuse the life-force, the sacred fire and the ascension flame to control and manipulate life and who offer individuals all of the kingdoms of this world, all of their black magic, all of their manipulation of others.

See to it, then, for the mighty threefold flame within you,

your mighty Christ, your I AM Presence is able to subdue even the manipulation of this light of Alpha and Omega. And as Saint Germain, my brother and my father, has told you, they will pay fully for every misuse of the science of God and the alchemy of his Word. Therefore does he sound the warning in his *Studies in Alchemy* that the science may never, never be misused with impunity.

Beware the Magnetism of the Aura of the Fallen Angels

Beware, then, the magnetism of the aura of those fallen angels who walk by the power of the misuse of the base-of-the-spine chakra, who even claim to take dictations from *me* by this power and these distorted sexual practices.

Blessed ones of the light, in the mastery you gain in the divine order that I have taught this day, you will discover that there is no need for tantric yoga. For when you raise the Kundalini fire, it is not by the sexual practices but by the lodestone of your mighty I AM Presence, by Christ in your heart who is the magnet for the consummation of that fire in the crown of life. And this fire is for the Deathless Solar Body, and it is the ascension flame.

In the name of Serapis Bey, I charge you, then, to give your calls upon those individuals and movements this day that would sweep the lightbearers out of the path of the Great White Brotherhood in America and other nations by the popularity of these ancient practices of the dark ones!

They shall not pass!

They shall not *pass!*

They shall not pass over the threshold of the bride and the Bridegroom! They shall not enter the marriage chamber of Christ and his beloved!

They shall not pass!

But the saints of God who follow the Lamb whithersoever he goeth, who follow the Christ by the fixing of the star of the attention upon the Bridegroom—the one hundred and forty and four thousand who move to the Mount Zion,[8] the place of the I AM Presence—they shall overcome, they shall inherit, they shall have the light of the Mother flame rising within them. They shall seal it in the third eye.

They, therefore, shall be called virgins—not of the flesh but of the Spirit. For the virgin within them is the virgin light *sealed* in the third eye! And therefore, they are not defiled by the Great Whore but are carried up, and their sin remaineth not but is consumed by the violet flame! And therefore, they are purified and made white—not of their own righteousness but of the Righteousness of the Lord who dwelleth in them.

What Fellowship Hath Light with Darkness?

See ye to it, my beloved, for it is the hour when the dark ones seek to manipulate even the ascension process. They would gain eternal life by mixing their seed, the seed of the godless, with the lightbearers. Take care, then, that you understand my word: What fellowship hath light with darkness?[9]

Realize that you may not partake either of the flesh, either of the synthetic image of the Cain civilization, lest you be caught in a long, long spiral of karma—a similar one that you now are ending by the power of the Great Divine Director given unto you for the arresting of the spirals of Death and Hell.

Have you forgotten that call of the Great Divine Director who has *empowered* you to arrest the spirals of unreality?[10] I bid you listen to that release this day that you might understand how to wield the mighty two-edged sword.

Watch and Pray—Beware of Sympathy and Pride

Therefore, take care that you do not, through sympathy, enter in anew into those associations that we have freed you from in these hours of your path. But move upward and receive, then, the joy of the resurrection flame. For this flame shall be unto you the quickening of light, the quickening of all momentums of God's goodness, God's attainment within you, until your strength is one with the strength of Christ.

And when you feel it and when you know it, then watch and pray; for the next awakening will be of the dweller. And thus, beforehand begin to pronounce the judgment I have given you this day that he might be significantly reduced even before he is awakened. Thus, there are strategies of light, you see, even as there are strategies in darkness.

And finally, when you have gotten that victory over the beast, the awakening will be of the ascension flame rising within you. And then you will know the meaning of the conquering ones—not the pride of those who condemn and condemn and condemn our messengers and our disciples worldwide. They know not the heart of our servant. They know not the heart of the chela.

I know your hearts, beloved. I know your hearts. Fear not, for I know your love. But only be concerned that that which sets itself against thy heart from beneath be taken and bound and cast into the fire by your conscious will, by your conscious devotion, before it put upon you any further burden.

Why do you suppose, blessed ones, there is the failing of men's hearts for fear?[11] It is because the heart becomes burdened by the toxic waste, if you will, the substance misqualified in the caldron of the electronic belt, and it rises against the heart chakra and the physical heart. And instead of pouring forth the balm of Gilead in Christ through that heart, instead of discovering the divine nectar of the crown by the union of the life-force of Alpha and Omega, instead of the violet flame, these individuals go after heart surgery, heart transplants—as though they could create a heart of life and of God.

What a pity, so much striving to discover the mechanical means to ascend, blessed ones—almost uncomprehensible! Yet more's the pity, this is all they have to hope for—the mechanical manipulation of life—hoping against all hope, indeed, that by material science alone they shall discover the fount of youth, they shall meet the mighty youth Sanat Kumara[12] or somehow know the state of grace. And how they suffer in their striving for their physical perfection!

All of this for what? What god do they serve? Surely not my Father and your Father, not my God and your God, beloved. Surely not the dharma of the Buddha. Surely not my way.

What god do they serve? Why, beloved, they serve the god they have made out of the dweller-on-the-threshold— enthroned and enshrined—the stony-faced god, the condemner of all people. You see, they stole the light of the Mother Goddess and endowed the dweller with life, and thus they attempt to perpetuate that dweller.

Many Long Ago Took the Left-Handed Path

Many in the world today long ago took the left-handed path, long ago enshrined that fallen one, you see. Their choices are long past. They do not stand where you stand at this portal of opportunity. They are old, old souls. This is why they are called laggards. This is why they have lived so long in other worlds and systems.

They laugh at the innocence and the simplicity of the

children of light, for they have long ago done away with any desire for religion or God. It has availed them nothing, as they have offered nothing unto him.

Thus, you see, some have sustained the not-self. By usurping that ascension flame, by usurping the Mother light of Lemuria that burned upon the altars there, they have discovered even how to tap the magnetism, the life-force at the center of the earth and in the heart of a living cell. And this they gather, and this they imbibe, and this they take in for the feeding of the beast.

The Day of Judgment Is at Hand

Now you understand why it is the day of vengeance,[13] why judgment is at hand. Those who have clearly set themselves in the seat of the scornful dweller, they—*they* now know their time is come, because my little ones and my brothers and sisters have chosen to become one with me, with my Christ and your Christ, with my mighty I AM Presence and your mighty I AM Presence.

You wonder why they could so perpetuate themselves so long, so steal the light of the Virgin so long. Well, beloved, it is because the sons of God must descend to their level for that judgment. It is because the children of the light must also have the opportunity to choose to live as Christ, to choose to slay the dweller, to choose to raise the life-force.

When all these right choices are made and you have overcome, then you stand, *then* you stand—then, you see, you stand. And the call of the judgment is *powerful* in you! For you have the power of heaven, your mighty I AM Presence, and of the Father; and you have the power of the earth, the sacred fire of the Kundalini, your Mother; and you have the power of Christ, as Alpha and Omega are one in your heart, because your soul has chosen to be with that heart and to merge with my own.

Thus, the cycles for the fulfillment of this generation cannot be fulfilled till all these things be fulfilled in you.[14] Now you understand at least another facet of the mystery of the diamond-shining mind of God and of how and why and wherefore you walk this earth and you are witnesses to these conditions.

When you look at planetary evil, when you look into the very teeth of the Watchers and the serpents who parade before you daily on the television screen, you must surely come to the place of the mature son of God who must say:

In my heart I know what I must do in order to rid the planet of the Evil One. I know that I must conquer where I am and not delay and not tarry! I know that I must overcome in God! And I know that He awaits my coming, that He might speak the Word through me of Judgment that will be finis— the end!—the final end of the doctrines of the wicked.

Why Evil Still Stalks the World—An Inescapable Reminder

Beloved hearts, if you would know the Truth, I would tell you that evil still stalks the world so that the good people who desire to follow me will have a perpetual and inescapable reminder that they have not yet slain their own carnal mind! And they have contented themselves to remain at the halfway point, satisfied to feed the beast and thereby tame it rather than starve it and slay it.

Many have made the choice to feed the beast, satisfy it with creature comforts and various addictions of the various chakras. But, beloved, choose not the way of all flesh[15]—and know that your victory is an individual and planetary victory and that the planetary dweller is reduced by the power and the magnitude of your overcoming of the energy veil within yourself. And ultimately everyone upon earth, if he would ascend, must slay the enemy within and the world consciousness of sin.

I have taught you, then, what is within your power to receive and to understand. Now, lest you be weary of so much light and exposure, I take my leave to the higher octaves of the New Jerusalem. I go to prepare a place for you at the Inner Retreat. And I AM with you always, even unto the end of your own self-created unreality.

For then, you see, we will be more than companions, we will be one—I AM THAT I AM.

"I CAST OUT THE DWELLER ON THE THRESHOLD!"
by Jesus Christ

In the name I AM THAT I AM ELOHIM,
  Saint Germain, Portia, Guru Ma, Lanello,
In the name I AM THAT I AM SANAT KUMARA,
  Gautama Buddha, Lord Maitreya, Jesus Christ,
I CAST OUT THE DWELLER ON THE THRESHOLD of
_____[name specific situations]_____.

In the name of my beloved mighty I AM Presence and
Holy Christ Self, Archangel Michael and the hosts of the
LORD, in the name Jesus Christ, I challenge the personal and
planetary dweller on the threshold, and I say:

You have no power over me! You may not threaten or mar
the face of my God within my soul. You may not taunt or
tempt me with past or present or future, for I AM hid with
Christ in God. I AM his bride. I AM accepted by the LORD.

You have no power to destroy me! Therefore, be bound!
by the LORD himself.

Your day is *done!* You may no longer inhabit this temple.

In the name I AM THAT I AM, be *bound!* you tempter of
my soul. Be *bound!* you point of pride of the original fall of
the fallen ones! You have no power, no reality, no worth. You
occupy no time or space of my being.

You have no power in my temple. You may no longer steal
the light of my chakras. You may not steal the light of my
heart flame or my I AM Presence.

Be *bound!* then, O Serpent and his seed and all implants of the sinister force, for *I AM THAT I AM!*

I AM the Son of God this day, and I occupy this temple fully and wholly until the coming of the LORD, until the New Day, until all be fulfilled, and until this generation of the seed of Serpent pass away.

Burn through, O living Word of God!

By the power of Brahma, Vishnu and Shiva, in the name Brahman: I AM THAT I AM and I stand and I cast out the dweller.

Let him be bound by the power of the LORD's host! Let him be consigned to the flame of the sacred fire of Alpha and Omega, that that one may not go out to tempt the innocent and the babes in Christ.

Blaze the power of Elohim!

Elohim of God—Elohim of God—Elohim of God

Descend now in answer to my call. As the mandate of the LORD—as Above, so below—occupy now.

Bind the fallen self! *Bind* the synthetic self! Be *out* then!

Bind the fallen one! For there is no more remnant or residue in my life of any, or any part of that one.

Lo, I AM, in Jesus' name, the victor over Death and Hell! (2x)

Lo, *I AM THAT I AM* in me—in the name of Jesus Christ—is *here and now* the victor over Death and Hell!

Lo! it is done.

You must not wait with trepidation the day of the awakening of the dweller, but run to greet that enemy. Fully clothed upon with the armour of God, give your Tube of Light and calls to Archangel Michael before saying this decree (see pages 210, 211).

CHAPTER SEVEN

Christ and the Dweller
A Perpetual Path of Victory

Elizabeth Clare Prophet

The Anti-Buddha Force on Planet Earth

We have spoken on a number of occasions of the force of the anti-Buddha in the world, the anti-Buddha being that which is anti-American, anti-I AM Race; for example, World Communism or the manipulation of our educational system, making it a force of humanism set against the Christ within the child. We have also spoken of that which moves against the Buddha as the drug culture, as rock music, that which would destroy the path of the Buddha—in other words, the false hierarchy and the false gurus, and their modus operandi.

The betrayal of the light of the Son of God by the not-self in each one of us is a link to this planetary force of anti-Buddha. It can be seen in the electronic belt (at the seat-of-the-soul chakra level) manifesting as a black sun-center—a literal vortex of darkness swallowing up the soul's light as it spins in a counter-motion to the rotation of the Great Causal Body. Unless bound and cast out by the fiat of Almighty God himself, this dweller will not stop agitating for the enslavement of the soul.

Getting at the Nucleus of the Not-Self

Jesus has given us a new and wondrous decree for this very purpose—the binding and the casting out of the dweller-on-the-threshold of this anti-Buddha force in all of its ramifications. Jesus explained to me that when we give the Judgment Call "They Shall Not Pass!" (see p. 144), and we are naming the oppressors of the people of God, we are focusing on the self-conscious awareness of the individual in his motives and actions to manipulate life against the purposes of the Godhead. But when we give the decree for the binding and the casting out of the dweller, we are getting at the core of the human creation that is in opposition to the Divine. We are getting at the nucleus of the anti-God, or the anti-Self, and demanding that it be bound.

This decree, "I Cast Out the Dweller-on-the-Threshold!" (see p. 112), is a step-up from the first judgment call dictated by Jesus. The latter involves the judgment of words and deeds, the judgment of actions, step by step. It may bring the judgment of returning karma to the individual for a single act, for a single embodiment, for a single momentum; whereas the decree on the dweller is for the binding and casting out of the entire conglomerate of the carnal mind coiled in the center of the electronic belt. It is the original seed of evil at its inception that has grown to the present hour from the point of its beginning anytime—millions of years ago, a hundred thousand years ago, five years ago.

The dweller-on-the-threshold is the focal point of the consciousness behind the human creation—the mind behind the manifestation. This term has been adopted by the Brotherhood because it conveys the meaning that it sits at the threshold of self-awareness where the elements of the subconscious cross the line from the unconscious to the conscious world of the individual, and the unknown not-self becomes the known. Once surfaced, the dweller has entered the realm of the conscious will where, through the decision-making faculties of mind and heart, the soul may choose to "ensoul" or to slay the components of this antithesis of the Real Self.

The Surfacing of the Dweller

I remember when on our way home from Ghana in 1972, we went to Scotland with our beloved Mark. We took a train to northern Scotland and went to Loch Ness. Loch Ness is a very deep body of water, the habitat of the legendary Loch Ness monster. The Loch Ness monster is supposedly a remnant of some prehistoric type of water beast, or "leviathan," as is mentioned in the Bible—it looks like a giant sea dinosaur that swims about. This Nessie, as they call her, is supposedly a female.

And so, people come from all over the world watching for the Loch Ness monster. I can remember how we drove round and round the loch looking for the Loch Ness monster, and the idea is that occasionally you can see its head peeping above the water.

Well, Mark said he saw it. I didn't see it. I missed it. But nevertheless, there are books printed with pictures that people supposedly have taken of Nessie. This goes back several hundred years that people have been watching for the Loch Ness monster.

Of course, the loch is very still; it's an inland body of water. And so, seeing it may mean seeing just a little sliver of its tail or a sliver of its head or a sliver of its back.

But that body of water, or any body of water, represents the emotional body, its surface being the line that is drawn between the conscious and the subconscious mind. Whatever is below the surface is below the surface of our awareness. We may get rumblings and soundings that it's there, but until it finally emerges and manifests itself in some way, we don't necessarily know the definition of the dweller-on-the-threshold —somehow the marks of identification are missing.

It's right there ready to come through the door of consciousness, but at that threshold, at the line separating the planes of awareness, the guardian action of the Christ mind, the holy angels and one's free will stand to prevent the dweller from actually surfacing and moving into action in our world.

When the Dweller Gets Out of Control

Now, there are individuals, of course, who do not stand guard; and therefore they become suddenly and ferociously the instrument of a "sea monster" that is out of control. And so, you see, the more people become psychologically disturbed and have divisions in the four lower bodies, the more they are apt to manifest aberrations by which the dweller may gain entrance to their world through the lever of the conscious mind.

They may be schizophrenic, they may be subject to hearing voices and carrying out anything from mayhem to ridiculous little pastimes that they repeat all day long—all of this being the surfacing of the dweller, mocking and taunting the soul in what then becomes compulsive behavior—drug, alcohol and sugar addictions, et cetera, or even demon possession, exacerbating crime, child molesting and every form of vice. Once in control of the conscious mind, the dweller takes over the whole house, attracting discarnates and demons that bring death and destruction to many innocent bystanders before the victim, himself but a tool of the sinister force, succumbs.

Supposedly, in our society, the difference between someone who is sane and someone who is insane would be the control or non-control of that Loch Ness monster, that dweller-on-the-threshold that dwells in the sublevels of the emotional body. The person who makes the conscious decision not to allow the carnal mind to vent itself in the ups and downs of life is sane because he, and not the beast, is in command.

However, many people are entirely dominated by the carnal mind and extremely sane at the same time, or at least sane-appearing. When you get to know them, you don't think they're quite sane, but they do manage to run banks and big businesses and all kinds of corporate enterprises on this planet; and the planet manages to survive, and we survive. And sometimes we wonder why and how it all works.

The Face-to-Face Confrontation

Well, there comes a time in the life of the individual who contacts the Path, the masters or their representatives when he comes face to face with Christ and anti-Christ: Christ in the person of the man of God and anti-Christ in the personal dweller-on-the-threshold within himself; and he may see both face to face.

Now this usually does not happen the very day of the encounter with the Great White Brotherhood, but by and by it does occur. And sometimes people manage to follow the masters and the Path and the teachings for many years without experiencing the confrontation. Either they avoid it or they try to avoid the appearance of having had the confrontation, but ultimately when the masters determine to do so, they will force the confrontation and force their chelas to make a choice between the Christ Self and the dweller.

This may occur at any time on the Path. Some people sense this, and therefore they avoid all contact with the Great White Brotherhood or its agents. They may even take up arms against it, thinking to thwart the Law and the inevitable Day of Reckoning.

This was so in the case of Saul on the road to Damascus. In this case, it was the Master Jesus who forced the encounter, and Saul was blinded in the alchemical process of the light confounding the darkness. Jesus made Saul choose between his dweller, the anti-Christ or anti-Self who was persecuting the Christians, and his Real Self personified and represented in the ascended master Jesus Christ.

When he chose his Lord, he chose the path of discipleship leading to individual Christhood. And the Master bound his dweller until he himself should slay it "in the last day" of his karma. Endued with the power of Christ in his guru Jesus, Saul, now called Paul (having put off the old man and put on the new), went forth to witness to the Truth that had set him free from his own momentum of human creation and the human mind that created it—the dweller-on-the-threshold.[1]

From his personal confrontation and conversion by the Lord, Paul was later able to tell the Romans with the conviction that comes only from experience: "To be carnally minded is death; but to be spiritually minded is life and peace. Because the carnal mind is enmity against God: for it is not subject to the law of God, neither indeed can be."[2]

Now, I know that some people who've been studying the teachings of the masters for years whom I've never met, faithful readers of the *Pearls of Wisdom* and faithful Keepers of the Flame who've never even been to a conference (perhaps they're aged, confined, or whatever), may or may not have had the confrontation. Some of these people are extremely advanced souls and some of them are not so advanced, but they are what you would call steady plodders. And God loves their constant hearts! The same is true of those who have come closer to the organization. So you find that on the Path, every individual is a very unique world.

The Role of the Messenger

My service to the Brotherhood is that of messenger. I do not preempt the masters' intensification of their ray or the withholding thereof upon an individual. I may be fully aware of an individual's level of Christ consciousness, not that they have necessarily externalized it, but I know it is there in potential, and day by day and year by year they are making that slow but surefooted progress of putting on the mantle of their Christhood.

I might also be aware, if the Holy Ghost chooses to reveal it to me, of the fact that a person has a considerable momentum on the creating and sustaining of the dweller-on-the-threshold and that he may not be doing too much about casting out that dweller or overcoming those momentums, but may instead be inclining towards the dweller, avoiding the messenger, making a wide circle, and dodging the encounter with the Christ in the master that would force him to bind his own dweller with the help of the guru.

Sometimes I will simply look in the other direction for years while this individual is thinking, perhaps, that he is actually getting away with not surrendering those baser elements to the Christ mind. The reason I do this is that it is not my place to preempt the encounter of your soul with the master who is your Initiator, be it Saint Germain or El Morya or Lanello.

Because I am so careful about not getting in the way of

this relationship, I find that the masters trick me. They have me go and tell someone to do something that I myself would not consider earthshaking—nothing that would really cause anyone a problem.

Sometimes when I do this, I find that, on the contrary, to the individual it is an enormous problem and it does result in the inevitable encounter with the master whose spokesman I am. The person becomes very angry with me, they challenge me and tell me that they are not going to meet this request; whereupon I say, "Well, if I'd known it would have been such a problem, I would not have even brought it up in the first place." But, of course, it's out, and therefore I have to stand on the fact that the Rock of Christ has been the testing of a soul without my realizing that I was sent to be the instrument of the mission.

On other occasions, I will be sent on a mission to deal with such situations and I know very well that it could be extremely touchy, and I'm prepared for the worst. And oftentimes the best happens—people make forward strides and are very grateful, and the circle of community is benefited.

So in the matter of Christ and the dweller, then, we all have an opportunity, which we are given in the meditation of our own heart, in the private, patient communion of God with us, little by little to make choices without being under the pressure of Joshua's immediate command: "Choose you this day whom ye will serve!"[3]

And so, we may spend years or even embodiments exercising our free will, because the Law is very gracious to us in allowing us to figure out this problem of our own being, enabling us to see clearly that we have some element of human creation, some character trait that we definitely do not like. We know we don't want it, we smash it every time we see it, it reappears now and then, we smash it again. God knows we're trying and we're not fooling, and he leaves us alone. He lets us conquer, he lets us overcome.

Indulging the Human Creation

Then there's the other situation where people will hide from God, will tarry, will procrastinate too long, and the Great Law says, "Thus far and no farther. You have indulged your human creation for thousands of years. You have acted out your rebellion against God for too many lifetimes, *and this time, this is it!* Your decision and your decree in this situation will be the telling one." And the master will challenge his chela: "Either you renounce your recalcitrance and make an about-face now, or you may no longer be considered a chela of the Great White Brotherhood."

This action is taken by the Great Law because the master has borne his chela's karma for the duration of certain centuries, and the cycles of his sponsorship of the chela are spent. He has no choice but to compel the chela to come up higher. If he does not respond, the master must leave him to his own devices until the day the chela chooses to stand, face and conquer on his own, and thereby earn the right to the master's grace once again.

If I happen to be involved in this confrontation, it is, of course, very trying for me, as we can well imagine it must also be for the master. I do as I am told, and I strive in my soul to be obedient and to be impersonal so that I am truly a messenger (rather than a teacher or a judge or a tester), conveying only that which is the will of the master as he is dealing with the chela.

The Example of Jesus: Slaying the Planetary Dweller

Then there is, of course, on down the road of self-mastery, the initiation that comes nigh the point of the crucifixion, when the individual has considerable Christ attainment as well as balanced karma and is required to slay that dweller totally and utterly.

Jesus could not have been on the cross had he not slain the dweller. As a matter of fact, his illustration of slaying the dweller was his wilderness confrontation with Satan three years before the crucifixion.[4] And that was the planetary dweller-on-the-threshold: Satan himself—the personification and sign of everyone's personal dweller.

Later the Son of God dealt with the planetary dweller again in his confrontation with the Watchers and the Nephilim[5]—the chief priests and Pharisees, the elders of the people and the powers of Rome. This was possible only because he had already slain the personal dweller. This is why he said, "The prince of this world cometh, and hath [findeth] nothing in me."[6]

So the planetary momentum of the dweller-on-the-threshold, i.e., the collective undefined unconscious of all evolutions of the planet, can and does move against the individual who has not yet slain his personal carnal mind. What this means is the obvious—that most people come under the influence of the mass consciousness daily. And the more they have conquered the wiles of their own not-self, the less influenced they will be by the ups and downs of world turmoil.

Nevertheless, the planetary momentum will tie into and activate the personal anti-Christ to catch off-guard even the souls nearest their victory over the beast; at that moment the individual must slay not only the personal carnal mind, but in so slaying it, drive back the planetary momentum and overcome the original Liar as well as the lie that the originator of evil has propagated in his seed.

The Y on the Path: The Point of Overcoming

Now, you may day by day resist the temptations of your carnal mind and of the planetary dweller, but you may not have completely slain the personal representative of the Evil One. Thus, there is a point of winning on each occasion of the overcoming, and then there is the point of winning ultimately because the entire beast has been slain.

Well, there comes a time when individuals on the Path have had the fullness of the teaching, the light, the masters and the love of the community. And that fullness is not gauged by years but by the evolution of the lifestream. It may be one year, it may be three years, it may be twenty years, it may be many embodiments.

But there comes a point when the individual has full awareness of the Christ in the masters, in the messenger, full awareness of what the darkness is and what the carnal mind is. And he must come to the place of deciding for or against his mighty I AM Presence, the Brotherhood, for or against the false hierarchy. This is known as the Y. The Y in the Path is the point of the initiation where one actually becomes Christ or Antichrist.

One may refuse to surrender that dweller—to bind it, slay it, and send it to judgment aforehand—i.e., before the soul must give its accounting to the Karmic Board at the conclusion of this life. Jesus taught this law of karma to Paul, who wrote of it to Timothy: "Some men's sins are open beforehand, going before to judgment; and some men they follow after."[7]

Instead of surrendering it at the Y, the initiate may, instead, embrace the dweller. Instead of eating the flesh and drinking the blood of the Son of God (assimilating the light of Alpha and Omega in the Body of Christ), he literally drinks the cup of the blasphemy of the fallen angels and eats at their board the infamy of their anti-Word.

By taking the *wrong way*, the initiate actually puts on, personifies, identifies with, and is now become the dweller-on-the-threshold incarnate. The soul and the cancer of the carnal mind have grown together and are no longer separable. Such an individual would then be on the *left-handed path*. His will, not God's, is supreme. An adept on the left-handed path is called a black magician.

These events may happen very quickly, even overnight. The opportunity for service to the master during which an individual walks the path of discipleship in grace as a follower of Christ, still enjoying the protection and the sponsorship of the Brotherhood, continues right up until the hour of decision.

One day one sees the chela as a part of the community and in the grace of the masters, enjoying Maitreya's Mystery School and the opportunity to balance through service, right deeds and decisions, the karma borne during his apprenticeship by the guru. But the next, the day of decision is upon him. The individual may be confronted at any level of his being, not necessarily *by* the messenger, although it may be *through* the messenger. And he may at that moment decide that he will not give in to his Lord and master. He will not bend the knee, he will not confess the supremacy in his life of his Holy Christ Self. Instead, he considers himself—his untransmuted willful self—to be that Christ.

Confusing the lower self for the Greater Self through his own self-created spiritual blindness, he enthrones the dweller-on-the-threshold in the place of his Holy Christ Self. His personality, his psyche, his stream of consciousness all flow into the not-self. Instead of saying, "I and my Father are One,"[8] he declares, "I and my ego are one," and it is so. Behold mechanization man! Behold Rudyard Kipling's "man who would be king" who meets his fate in the abyss of the astral plane. Though he thinks he is in control, the nonentity eventuates in nonexistence.

This Is Your Hour and the Power of Darkness

Now this is happening on planet Earth every day to people who have chosen to embody the anti-Buddha force. These are advanced initiations, but then, planet Earth is host to very old souls whose hour has come. As Jesus said to the chief priests, the elders and captains of the temple who could have chosen Christ but, in murdering him, solidified their position with Satan and made their whole house his: "This is your hour"—to choose to be or not to be in the Christ consciousness—"and the power of darkness,"[9] i.e., the power of the darkness of your own dweller-on-the-threshold and your karma. "Now I, the One Sent, charge you to bind and cast out that carnal mind which is enmity with God, if you would dwell forevermore with the Father and the Son."[10]

Jesus' incarnation of the Word forced the confrontation, the choice and the judgment of these ancient ones who knew full well at all levels of their consciousness who he was and who they were. And in their hour, they made their choice. It was a fair test, fair and square, and they failed it.

Likewise, your Holy Christ Self will force the confrontation, the choice and the judgment not only of the dark ones, but of your own soul as well. Let us therefore judge righteous judgment. For we know, beloved, that with what measure we mete justice unto one another, it shall be meted upon our own heads from on high. The Law does not fail to reward each one, mercy for mercy.

It is very burdensome to our hearts to see anyone reject Reality for unreality. But this is not new to us. We have observed over the years betrayers of the light in all walks of life turn into the darkest of darkness overnight and become archdeceivers of innocent hearts.

When People Embody Their Dweller

These people, therefore, have become their dweller-on-the-threshold. They no longer even *pretend* to follow the true teachings of Christ taught by the Brotherhood. They deny that the teachings are true, they deny that the masters are real, and they deny the path of initiation under Maitreya through the embodied guru.

And what's more, they embrace a false doctrine of Christ's accountability for their sin—for all past sins of all previous lives, mind you—saying, "Jesus died for my sins, I am free from all my karma. I am exonerated. There is nothing I can or should do to balance my debts to life. My belief is my passport to the kingdom."

It is of no concern to them that they are in the very act of karma-making. In fact, they have so personified the dweller, and they are so pleased to be free to indulge that dweller with all its appetites and vehemence against the Law of Life, that they are either unconcerned or else unaware that they are on a collision course with destiny.

This cycling out of the planes of actuality into "outer darkness" or the self-extinguishment of the "second death"—two very specific doctrines of Jesus that cannot be rationalized away by the fallen ones[11]—may take many, many cycles according to cosmic law. The point here, which is made eloquently by Paul, is that the Adamic man cannot survive—neither here nor in the hereafter, unless he becomes the spiritual man, renewed, Spirit-filled, and walking in full communion with God.

In the meantime, the "ex-disciple" of Christ who is now

the servant of the natural man[12]—its wants and pleasures and superior knowledge—fashions a strong outer personality made in the likeness of the carnal mind—a 'good human being', achieving and acceptable in the circles of all who likewise have abandoned the road of eternal accountability that leads inevitably to the confrontation with Christ and the surrender of all sin against the Holy Ghost.

The Schism in the Psyche between Christ and the Dweller

This is an altogether simplistic and temporary resolution of the schism between Christ and the dweller that yet exists within the psyche. This avoidance of accountability for one's actions and for the decision not to slay the dweller at the Cross and the crossroads of life is indulged by the false pastors and their false doctrine of salvation. While perfunctorily and intellectually observing the rites of worship, they tolerate everyone's carnal mind, including their own, and fail to present the real challenge of the path of personal Christhood that Jesus taught.[13]

This decree, "I Cast Out the Dweller-on-the-Threshold!" has to do, then, with the confrontation—by those students of light who have chosen the path of discipleship under Jesus Christ or one of the ascended masters—with embodied individuals who have elected by free will to merge with their own carnal mind in rejection of Christ and his messenger— whoever that one who comes in the name of the Lord may be—and to become, in fact, the dweller.

These sincere students may not have come to the Y themselves. They may be God's precious children who have not the attainment to fully incarnate the Christ. They may not be at that point of Christic initiation. They may not be a Christed one who has the ability either to fight the personal or planetary dweller or to defend himself against the Antichrist.

Nevertheless, these dedicated souls are in fact being confronted and moved against by those self-serving ones who have embodied the dweller-on-the-threshold yet cleverly disguise themselves as benign, concerned citizens working for the freedom of all. Jesus tagged them so we would not be fooled by their too kind words: "wolves in sheep's clothing," devils posing as deliverers. And there is more truth to those words than many are prepared to deal with.

You see, the one who embodies that dweller—being self-willed, and inordinately imposing his will on others (this is the base definition of black magic), having passed the point of the Y—is actually incarnating that momentum of evil that is the equivalent of the light he had when he departed from the temple and fell from grace. In other words, he has inverted his original dispensation of light to generate evil. Moreover, he has deified that evil and himself as its progenitor.

The Liar and His Lie—the Nature of Evil

Evil, in itself, is misqualified energy, the malintent behind it, and the entity encompassing both. By the very nature of the Liar and his lie—the consciousness behind it—evil at its inception is deceptive and deceitful. In fact, it is a veil of illusion—an energy veil, or *e-veil,* enshrouding the Deity and all his marvelous works. Illusion, or *maya,* as the Hindus call it, then appears more real than Reality itself. In fact, men's illusions become their gods, and evil is deified.

Now, what is plain to see is that a devil *(d-evil)* is one who has deified evil and the entire energy veil. A devil is one who has deified the dweller-on-the-threshold to the position of Christ and has declared himself master and saviour of the world, whether in politics or art, or in the philosopher's chair or at the head of the PLO, the Baader-Meinhof gang, or in the Pentagon.

A devil is the Adamic man self-proclaimed as a messiah by his own ego energy in the place of salvation by The Lord Our Righteousness. Thus, we have those who deify the energy veil of the dweller posing as the deliverers of the race—and if we follow them instead of "Christ in you, the hope of glory,"[14] we shall all fall into the ditch that empties into the River Styx. May the Lord enlighten you as to who and what we are dealing with and why you need to give these calls *every day!*

Now, since the one who embodies the dweller, thereby deifying evil, may have been a Watcher or a fallen angel (Lucifer was an archangel who fell through pride, as we know), the attainment at the point of the Fall may have been very great—for these fallen ones once had a great light, dwelling as they did in the courts of heaven with our Father and Mother. So the greater the light at the point of the Fall, the greater the Fall, and the longer the extension of time and space in which to repent. For God, in his truly great mercy, gives to that one an opportunity commensurate with his office in hierarchy at the time of the Fall to repent and to return to him.

Those who once had great light may be given even a longer opportunity to balance their karma and return to the throne of grace than those who had less. This is a corollary to the law of karma, as it is written: For he that hath, to him shall be given; and he that hath not, from him shall be taken even that which he hath.[15]

How Long, O Lord?

And so, we know that the opportunity given to some of the fallen ones has been very, very, *very* long, until even the

Psalmist thousands of years ago cried out, "How long, O LORD, how long will the wicked triumph?"[16] For the power of their dweller-on-the-threshold seems endless as they move against the children of God who seem so much less powerful and often helpless.

Indeed, the fallen angels who swore their eternal enmity against God in heaven—in the full presence of his glory!—move freely on earth, embodying the dweller with bravado, sophistication, wealth and worldly wisdom until they should be confronted by someone in embodiment—someone who has the courage to be the spokesman for the Elect One. For by definition, by the very science of being, that Elect One who cometh in the name of the LORD I AM THAT I AM has the attainment of light physically manifest equal to the dark ones; the One Sent did not fall from grace but took incarnation for the express purpose of challenging the seed of the wicked on behalf of the shorn lambs of God.

This is why John the Baptist and Jesus Christ as well as the prophets and the avatars of all ages have come to the earth: "For judgment I am come into this world."[17] They come because they want to give a reprieve to the blessed children of God who are tormented by these fallen ones and yet have not the ability—the externalized Christ consciousness—to move against them.

The Science of the Spoken Word for Judgment

Now in this hour of the Aquarian age and the dispensation of Saint Germain, we find that by the Science of the Spoken Word, when we give our dynamic decrees in the name of the Christ, in the name of the entire Spirit of the Great White Brotherhood or any of the ascended masters, we are decreeing in the full magnitude of their attainment sealed in their causal body of light.

When you decree in the name of Saint Germain, instantaneously you have behind your call the full power of the light qualified by the ascended master Saint Germain for thousands of years. His purple fiery heart multiplies the power of your heart, and it is as though Saint Germain and you were one. In fact, you *are* one.

Therefore, when you confront the Adversary within or without, you know that Saint Germain has the equivalent or greater of the power, let's say, of the archangel (or any other fallen one) when he fell. And therefore, Saint Germain is able to fulfill the decree of the Word through you, even if your own externalized light is not adequate to the encounter with Antichrist.

This is why little children of the light, those who've not balanced the threefold flame, those who have recently come into the teachings of the ascended masters, may in Jesus' name give his decree for the binding and casting out of the dweller-on-the-threshold and, as representatives of the Elect One, become a part of our concerted efforts to move against world situations of organized crime, war, massive forcefields of negative energy, problems in the economy—which to a great extent are controlled by Watchers and fallen ones who long ago chose to embody the dweller-on-the-threshold and have actually gone unchallenged (in *this* physical octave, i.e., on *this* earth) since the last Christed one appeared.

As a result of the dispensation of Jesus' judgments, his call to our Father and his Presence with us whereby we may now indeed challenge by Christ's power the evildoers, we are seeing unprecedented planetary changes. The fallen ones are shocked and affrighted. They cannot believe that they could be challenged and that the light—or the 'light-bearer'—could win, so accustomed are they to look down upon and to

CHRIST AND THE DWELLER | 133

control by intimidation the children of God who do not have nearly the momentum on creating Good that they have on creating Evil. (That is, the children of God do not have on the right-handed path of Light—of Absolute Good—the momentum that the fallen ones have on the left-handed path of Darkness—of Absolute Evil.) But then, they never really counted on the Faithful and True saving the day for the LORD and his anointed!

At whatever point the reprobate decided to embody the dweller, at that point on the Path he inverted the light he had acquired up to that moment. If he succeeded in stealing the fruit of the tree of the knowledge of good and evil, and was not then and is not now challenged by a son of God, he will go on misappropriating the light, turning it to greater darkness—"If the light that is in thee be darkness, how great is that darkness!"[18] Thus, he practices karma-dodging by devices of deceit, fooling the children of the light, inciting them to accuse one another, to argue with each other, to be discordant, to engage in wars and genocide in defense of Nephilim divide-and-conquer political schemes, and generally to get into a heap of troubles.

Be Wise as Serpents and Harmless as Doves

This inequity between the children of light and the children of this world (the seed of Christ and the seed of the Watchers and Nephilim) led Jesus to admonish: "The children of this world are in their generation wiser than the children of light.... Be ye therefore wise as serpents and harmless as doves."[19]

Making karma by their foolishness, putting their attention upon the fallen ones through idolatry, the children of light unwittingly give them their energy. (It is the law of karma: that which we place our attention on, or give our devotion to, we become; i.e., energy flows to the object of our attention and devotion.)

The fallen ones make a spectacle of themselves, preferring politics, the media and entertainment as center stage. Focusing our attention on their outrageous, hilarious or spectacular antics, they rake in our money and our light. And therefore, a fallen one walking the earth today as the incarnate dweller-on-the-threshold, though spiritually bankrupt, may actually be gathering more power and more light unto himself, which he turns into darkness to control and destroy the very ones from whom he has taken it by the schemes he has perpetrated.

Many of these schemes center on money, because money is power. Money, even if it's paper, represents gold; it represents energy, it represents supply, the abundance of God, and it has a worth that is determined solely by the sacred labor of the people and by their trust. "In God we trust."

When money is amassed by those who have chosen to embody the dweller instead of Christ, that means power. Money and power are necessary coordinates of control. It is plain to see that the 'serpents' (a scriptural term for embodied fallen angels who have misqualified the Kundalini,[20] the 'serpent force', to control others through the misuse of the chakras) have used their power, gained as money, to turn world conditions and world events toward themselves and to propagate after their kind. And so, as like attracts like, their offspring are also those who have chosen to embody the dweller-on-the-threshold.

Thus the dynasties of the powered and moneyed interests carry on "the tradition," reincarnating until the law of cycles decrees their judgment by the sons of God, ascended and unascended. And so the cycles of manipulation continue until the one aligned with the Great White Brotherhood raises his right hand, lifts up his voice unto the LORD God, the Almighty

One, and says: "In the name of Jesus Christ, Thus far and no farther! Enough!" and then gives the decree for the binding and the casting out of the dweller-on-the-threshold of the manipulators of the people.

They Shall Not Pass! The Judgment of Jesus

Jesus deliberated before giving us this dictation and this decree. Having given to us the decree "They Shall Not Pass!" in his dictation of August 6, 1978, he wanted to be certain we would be ready and unshakable in our faith and God-determination to see through the next phase of the judgment call. So you see how many years our Master has been testing us in our use of his fiat.

It is out of the sacred trust he holds with us, and we with him, in the correct use of the judgment calls by the greater number of the devotees, that the Son of God Jesus the Christ gives to us a much more incisive and powerful call through his name and vibration—his Electronic Presence and causal body multiplying our words by his Word.

It is a very important call because when we say, "I cast out the dweller-on-the-threshold," we're talking about the personal and planetary dweller, we're talking about everyone on earth in or out of embodiment who has raised a clenched fist to dare the Almighty to strike him dead, everyone who has hated the light, declared war against the Faithful and True, and spilled the blood of his sons and daughters in the rites and revenge of hell.

Whoever the perpetrators of evil are (and we ourselves need not know), the angels of the Lord Christ—the legions of the archangels and of Elohim—bind and render inactive the core of Absolute Evil within them and all that which is aligned with it. This is the true and righteous judgment that cleaves asunder the Real from the unreal, thereby opening the door to salvation to millions of oppressed peoples worldwide, and saving the world from the ultimate revenge of the false gods: planetary holocaust.

It is our earnest prayer that those whose ungodly deeds are challenged by our call—even those allied with nefarious practices—might be liberated from the strong delusions of the dweller and make an about-face to serve the living God. In giving this call, we are the champions of the soul and the defenders of the right of the individual to be free from the sinister strategies of the carnal mind—free to be his Real Self. This is a rescue mission on behalf of all caught in the grips of the illusions of the astral plane and its denizens.

This call is Jesus' sword. With it he goes forth to save the "lost sheep of the house of Israel" who have fallen into the cult of success, status, hedonism and excessive materialism. With all of his heart's love, our Master asks us to pray without ceasing for those who cannot see that they are enslaved by their own indulgence in the not-self. And see they must, before they can believe. Lord, heal them of their spiritual selfishness and its effect: spiritual blindness!

This, my beloved, is the increase of the Christ consciousness on earth. The Judgment Call and the dweller decree are given by the Son of God as the signal to his angels that the consummation of the age of Pisces is at hand and the harvest of the tares sown among the wheat is nigh.

It is time for the bands of angels known as the Reapers to gather the seed of the children of the Wicked One sown among the good seed of the Son of man.[21] When both calls dictated by beloved Jesus are combined with calls to the Elohim Astrea, Archangel Michael, the decree to "Reverse the Tide" and the violet flame, you will find that the archangels can move in to do a wondrous work for God and his children of light on earth!

I am therefore very joyous to have these instruments of the will of God, and I wanted to be certain that you would understand just how powerful are these dictations and decrees by the ascended master Jesus Christ.

We see that by the lineage of the path of discipleship, the saints have the mantle and the dispensation for the judgment not only of the fallen angels whose hour has come, but also of those among the twelve tribes who have committed themselves to their cause. It is written in the Bible that Jesus said, "The Father judgeth no man, but hath committed all judgment unto the Son."[22] And the Son Jesus has given that authority for the judgment to the apostles through the Holy Christ Self. Read for yourself:

> Do ye not know that the saints shall judge the world? and if the world shall be judged by you, are ye unworthy to judge the smallest matters? Know ye not that we shall judge angels? how much more things that pertain to this life?[23]
>
> And Jesus said unto them, Verily I say unto you, That ye which have followed me, in the regeneration when the Son of man shall sit in the throne of his glory, ye also shall sit upon twelve thrones, judging the twelve tribes of Israel.[24]
>
> Ye are they which have continued with me in my temptations. And I appoint unto you a kingdom, as my Father hath appointed unto me, that ye may eat and drink at my table in my kingdom and sit on thrones judging the twelve tribes of Israel.[25]
>
> And when he had said this, he breathed on them, and saith unto them, Receive ye the Holy Ghost: Whose soever sins ye remit, they are remitted unto them; and whose soever sins ye retain, they are retained.[26]

The Tools to Overcome Evil—
The Call Compels the Answer

The problem with Christianity today is that the children of the light are not being given the tools to obey Christ's injunction: Be not overcome of the Evil One but overcome the power of Evil with the power of Good.[27] While the world hangs in the balance of the arms race and war on every hand, the sword of the Saviour—the Science of the Spoken Word—is waiting to be wielded by all sons of God on earth for the binding of planetary evil and those who are its perpetrators.

How else shall we save the world, my beloved, without resorting to the unlawful methods of the fallen ones? The Call compels the answer! And the answer is always the true and righteous judgment of the LORD. Our will cannot interfere with these calls. The law of the Mediator guarantees that every prayer offered in the name of Jesus Christ—in the name of his Christ and our Christ, his God (I AM Presence) and our God (I AM Presence)—is weighed in the heart of the Advocate, aligned with the Father's will and answered accordingly.

The fact of Christ's intercession in all Christian prayer can be noted from James: "Ye ask, and receive not, because ye ask amiss [evilly], that ye may consume it upon your lusts."[28] This shows that the power of the spoken Word belongs to Christ and that if our word does not conform to his Word, it is not invocative of a heavenly response. In fact, when inordinate, our word is stopped at the level of the Mediator, our Holy Christ Self, and can go no higher.

If our call is ungracious, it cannot reach the throne of grace of our I AM Presence whose All-Power is the source of the answered call. Instead, The Lord Our Righteousness sends the call back to us with instruction on how we should pray, what our motive and heart should be, and how we must correct our vibration. If we are receptive, teachable and self-correcting, we can purify our words and intent and try again.

John also taught the law of God's will as a prerequisite to righteous prayer: "Whatsoever we ask, we receive of him, because we keep his commandments, and do those things that are pleasing in his sight.... This is the confidence that we have in him, that, if we ask any thing according to his will, he heareth us."[29]

Worlds without end, the Call accelerates the cycles of returning karma. This karma must reach the doorstep of the individual sometime, somewhere. Jesus has told me that he has given us the Judgment Call and the dweller decree so that he may in his greater wisdom (far greater than our poor power to adjudicate the affairs of earth) fulfill his prophecy through us and all of his disciples on earth concerning the shortening of the days for the elect.

You recall that the Master said, "Except those days should be shortened, there should no flesh be saved: but for the elect's sake those days shall be shortened."[30] Jesus has interpreted the term "shortening of the days" to mean the acceleration of the cycles—whether of the judgment of the seed of the Wicked One or of the resurrection of the elect (the representatives of the Elect One).

Something Must Be Done

Surely it is not difficult to see in world events, day by day, that something must be done. If those bent on world destruction are not bound by the hosts of the LORD and brought to judgment and if the lightbearers are not resurrected from the lethargy of the carnal mind to the wakefulness of the Christ mind in its vigil for world freedom, then it is entirely possible that "no flesh should be saved."

By facing their returning karma head-on, those who have gone astray or fallen asleep can learn quickly from their mistakes, make amends, and return to right mindfulness and right action before the whole mountain of their karma should descend upon them, effectively destroying their opportunity for another chance to "do it right" in their present embodiment. The Judgment Call and the dweller decree bless the giver and the receiver, liberating both from layers of unreality —scar tissue of bygone traumas that must be cleared for the soul's resurrection in Christ.

The Blessing of the Judgment in Our Own World

In giving these invocations, you must be prepared, beloved, for whatever you send forth to also activate the light in your own world. The judgment of the Son of God is the greatest blessing that anyone who loves the LORD could ever receive. It is like a pre-exam or a midterm before the final that lets us know where we stand vis-à-vis God's Laws. When we know where we stand, and what we know and what we don't know, what is pleasing and what is not pleasing to God, we can then study, correct and perfect our understanding and our actions, so that when the final examination comes, we will pass.

I want you to know that I ask God to judge my soul daily, and his angels to rebuke my errors, to teach me and to show me the way to do better. I give no power to the enemy's judgments of my life and work, but I do implore the Holy Spirit to analyze all constructive criticism, of friend and foe alike, and set before me the will of God for necessary change and progress in my soul and in our church.

Now, in this very moment of Jesus' dispensation from our beloved Father to have his Electronic Presence over everyone in whom there burns a certain measure of the threefold flame, we realize that when we give these prayers in Jesus' name, we are automatically saying them in the name of the Christ Self of everyone with whom Jesus is one through this new dispensation.

"The power of God through faith unto salvation" is limitless.[31] We must see it as such, and we must be relentless to deal with the entrenched forces of anti-Christ within individuals, organizations, councils, nations, bankers, et cetera. Whatever the conditions that are anti-Buddha, anti-Christ, anti–Great White Brotherhood or anti-Truth—anti–the little children—on the planet, this is where we go. And we go to it every time there is opposition to the absolute God-freedom of every living soul to pursue the path of Saint Germain.

This is our vow—no more, no less—to stand with and for the Truth spoken by Thomas Jefferson: "I have sworn upon the altar of God, eternal hostility against every form of tyranny over the [Christ] mind of man."[32]

So I think by calling upon the LORD with perfect love, the perfect ruby ray (i.e., blood of Christ), without anger, animosity or revenge or any vibration less than Christ Truth—for these are no part of the initiates of the sacred fire—we will see God's justice, and not our own, prevail on earth as it is in heaven.

The Prophecy of Daniel Is Being Fulfilled

This is the hour of the fulfillment of the prophecy of Daniel:

> And at that time shall Michael stand up, the great prince which standeth for the children of thy people; and there shall be a time of trouble, such as never was since there was a nation even to that same time. And at that time thy people shall be delivered, every one that shall be found written in the book.
>
> And many of them that sleep in the dust of the

earth shall awake, some to everlasting life, and some to shame and everlasting contempt.

And they that be wise shall shine as the brightness of the firmament; and they that turn many to righteousness as the stars for ever and ever.[33]

This is the hour of the awakening of the sleeping serpent of the dweller-on-the-threshold; this is the hour of judgment for those who choose not to be God but to be the embodiment of evil; this is the hour of the judgment of *many* who have chosen the left-handed path, many who have become one with Antichrist, many who have inverted the light to create the monster.

This is the hour when Jesus Christ has sent forth his call to the Father to bind them and cast them into the outer darkness, the astral plane, which they themselves have created; for these fallen ones are the creators of that Death and Hell that itself shall be cast into the Lake of Sacred Fire.

We know not how God will accomplish his purpose or how the holy angels will implement the judgments of the Son. We have no desire to see anyone go through a physical death or even the second death: this is not the purpose of the Judgment Call or the dweller decree! It is for the life of the soul in the grips of the toiler that we cry out to God for salvation through his great and marvelous works—beginning with his perfect judgment.

Jesus' prayers are life-giving, not death-inducing. They are the fulfillment through his disciples in the ending of Pisces and the beginning of Aquarius of his eternal reason for being: "I AM come that they might have life and that they might have it more abundantly."[34] To have life and that in full abundance, we need the sacred fire, the all-consuming fire of our God[35] to consume the shroud of death. And that's all the dweller is—the mask of death you tear off on Halloween and cast into the freedom flame.

We are charged to make the call, and the armies of heaven under the archangels are charged to implement the answer, subject to the will of God and the adjudication of the Son, in Jesus and in us. Praise God that only the will of Christ can manifest, and that neither our human opinion nor anyone else's can alter the divine edict that was spoken by the Father in the beginning and is ratified by the Son in the ending.

We are sons of God; we work on the yellow ray of Christ-illumination. The Elohim work on the blue, power ray of the Father, and the angels work on the pink ray of the Holy Spirit. The three are one through their universal devotion to the Cosmic Virgin. If we fulfill our office through the mind of God, the angels will perform their work through his love, and the Elohim and the elementals will perform theirs through his supreme edicts. We need only be certain that we invoke the necessary protection from the hosts of the LORD in our daily service and decrees.

THE JUDGMENT CALL
"THEY SHALL NOT PASS!"
by Jesus Christ

In the name of the I AM THAT I AM,
    I invoke the Electronic Presence of Jesus Christ:
They shall not pass!
They shall not pass!
They shall not pass!
By the authority of the cosmic cross of white fire
    it shall be:
That all that is directed against the Christ
    within me, within the holy innocents,
    within our beloved messengers,
    within every son and daughter of God...
Is now turned back
    by the authority of Alpha and Omega,
    by the authority of my Lord and Saviour Jesus Christ,
    by the authority of Saint Germain!
I AM THAT I AM within the center of this temple
    and I declare in the fullness of
    the entire Spirit of the Great White Brotherhood:
That those who, then, practice the black arts
    against the children of the light...
Are now bound by the hosts of the Lord,
Do now receive the judgment of the Lord Christ
    within me, within Jesus,
    and within every ascended master,

Do now receive, then, the full return
    multiplied by the energy of the Cosmic Christ
    of their nefarious deeds which they have practiced
    since the very incarnation of the Word!
Lo, I AM a Son of God!
Lo, I AM a flame of God!
Lo, I stand upon the rock of the living Word
And I declare with Jesus, the living Son of God:
They shall not pass!
They shall not pass!
They shall not pass!
    Elohim. Elohim. Elohim. [chant]

CHAPTER EIGHT

The Personal and Planetary Consciousness of the Dweller-on-the-Threshold

Elizabeth Clare Prophet

God has placed a bouquet of roses in my heart to bring to you today, and I'm very happy to do so. So won't you sit back and enjoy this wondrous teaching of Lord Himalaya.[1]

By way of introducing my subject, I would like to recount to you an incident that occurred this week when I had to attend a business luncheon. In the course of the conversation, a person who appreciates the teachings but is not a member of our activity said, "You know, So-and-so" (and he was speaking of someone who was a leader of a New Age movement), "So-and-so said to me that it's a wonderful work you're doing and he could well understand if this work were done in the name of the inspiration of God, but the thing that really turns him off is all of these other people, like Saint Germain and Archangel Gabriel and Jesus and El Morya. He couldn't quite understand this, because, he said, 'You know, you and I just go directly to God, so why does she have to go through all of these other people in order to get to God?' "

Well, this is a very interesting fallacy. And it's the fallacy of Protestantism—the protest movement of the Protestants moving against the communion of the saints.

So I said to him, "If this is So-and-so's theory, then he should sit home and not talk to anyone else but God. There's no reason for me to be having lunch with you today as my friend if there's no reason for us to talk to anyone else but God."

And so I said, "Archangel Michael is my friend, that's why I talk to him. And you are my friend; that's why I'm talking with you and eating lunch with you."

The Communion of Saints

And then I told him about the day that I was walking alone in Santa Barbara and I decided to go and get a bite to eat in a restaurant. And as I was walking along, Archangel Gabriel came up alongside of me and walked with me. And he came into the restaurant with me and sat down with me and he said to me, "I want you to conduct a seminar in San Francisco, and I want you to call it 'Portals of Purity.' "

I got out my little piece of paper, and he dictated to me the program for that particular seminar. I held it. It was kind of an odd sort of name. People around me protested this name, "Portals of Purity," but I said, "Archangel Gabriel gave me the name."

So we held that seminar, and it was a seminar of great rejoicing to many. And, of course, portals of purity are your own chakras—open doors to purity. And the exercise of the violet flame, and so forth, leads to that purity.

I said to the friend at lunch, "You see, Archangel Gabriel talks to God, I talk to God, and we talk to each other!" And so this is what friends ought to do, Above and below.

It's a very interesting thing that people think it's all well and good to talk to one another on earth, but as soon as you start talking to saints in heaven instead of talking to God, there's something wrong with your perception of the straight line that we all ought to have to the Almighty.

Well, of course, we understand and we should remember that the saints carry a tremendous momentum of devotion. And they can give us that momentum when we understand that because they are one with Christ, they may enhance and multiply and be transformers. We may possess a grain of truth; they may have a mountain. And they're very happy to multiply our grain by the mountain of their momentum.

The Neutralization of Hierarchy

It is a wondrous experience to commune with the saints. But the unfortunate part about this story is that millions of people who are Protestants have been taught, since Martin Luther manifested his rebellion, that there is no point of going through anyone to get to God—which is actually an act of defiance.

It's like saying, "I refuse to speak to anyone in this company but the chairman of the board." You want to go to the bank and withdraw twenty dollars? "I demand the president of this bank come down here and give me my twenty dollars! I will not talk to you, you clerk at the window."

It is an act of defiance: "I will not submit to the Son of God, or the Son of God in the many saints of heaven, but I will only speak with God, and I will only take my directions from him."

Therefore, it is the neutralization of hierarchy—the hierarchy of Elohim and archangels and ascended masters. God has set them in their offices, holy offices of service, so that we might benefit from their momentum and so that God himself may tend to the business that he tends to and we may learn from teachers who are closer to our evolution.

God, in fact, occupies the point of the mighty I AM Presence, and in the absolute sense of Brahman, has no awareness of maya, illusion or evil or the energy veil. This is why it says in the Bible that the Father has given unto the Son the entire matter of the judgment of the fallen ones.[2] The Father has authorized and set up the hierarchical office that the Son of God—the Christ, the Universal Christ, and the Christ in Jesus, and finally, the Holy Christ Self of you—is that point of discrimination that discerns good and evil and makes decisions concerning the embodiment of evil. This is why Jesus, therefore, because he had that mantle, as he broke bread and gave communion, conferred to his apostles the authority of judging the twelve tribes and the fallen angels.

You understand hierarchy and you understand the Trinity and offices of God if you simply think about it. Brahman, the point of God that knows only light and is only light, the point where the Word comes forth, that point of consciousness must be sustained on Absolute Good and on magnifying that Absolute Good within you and within me. That is the position of the I AM Presence.

When evolutions fell into valleys of illusion and compromise and relative good and evil, God sent forth his beloved Son into the world, that through that Son the world might be saved. God sent forth the Christ consciousness out of his heart to gather up our soul and our being that we might return. God has assigned to your Great Mediator and mine, to the Christ Self, the task of teaching us, instructing us, showing us right and wrong, chastening us, spanking us when we need it, keeping us on the right path. It is the divine office of the Son to so do.

And while the Son does this, the Father maintains the

immaculate concept of the whole creation and the immaculate concept of your return to him; whereas the Christ Self is very near the struggle and the overcoming and is aware of and knows what is the condition of error in our consciousness.

Your Christ Self: The Voice of God Speaking in Your Heart

The idea, therefore, of talking only to God becomes a myth. Because when the untransmuted consciousness that is in a state of maya and illusion addresses Almighty God, God answers through the Christ Self. When you call to your mighty I AM Presence and a voice responds to you, it is the voice of the Son translating the all-powerful light emanation of the Presence for a specific direction in your life.

So even when people say, "I only talk to God," the response from God comes from a point of the Christ consciousness—whatever point of that Christ consciousness is needed by that one. The point of that Christ consciousness could as easily be Lord Himalaya or Jesus Christ or Gautama Buddha or an ascended master or a saint that we have never heard of; but that voice of that one who can answer the individual's needs is delivered to the heart, to the seat of the conscious mind, and to the soul through the individual's Christ Self.

When you hear the voice of God speaking in your heart and in your temple, it is the voice of your Christ Self, who may, however, be delivering the message of El Morya or Saint Germain or the mighty I AM Presence or Padma Sambhava.

It's very important that we understand that if God were to leave the point of Absolute Being and Absolute Perfection to engage in the turmoil of illusion, then the Almighty One, the Infinite One, would, in fact, be leaving the great throne of the Absolute, and the universe would collapse.

The understanding of Brahman is the understanding of what Buddha called the "undifferentiated suchness," the pure point of God without quality. Out of the absolute Brahman comes forth the Word, which is the power of the whole creation. Out of Brahman comes forth a Trinity, and the Trinity is three persons that represent to us God—God the Father, God the Son, God the Holy Spirit.

You must realize that in the individualized focus of Almighty God, in the very heart of the I AM Presence, there is the Sun behind the sun that represents Brahman. And out of Brahman comes forth the image or the face of Brahma, which is Father; Vishnu, Son; and Shiva, the Holy Spirit.

So we can walk and talk with God the Father, God the Son and God the Holy Spirit as persons. But behind the three is that point of God that does not enter into our movements, our comings and goings and the sine wave of our experiencing good and evil in this world of time and space.

When we understand this, we realize that when any of the ascended masters is speaking to us, that one is speaking to us through the Trinity as either Father, Son, Holy Spirit or Mother —or as all four in one—as God ordains for each of us to have the full attainment of the four persons of the Godhead. The very fact that God is speaking means that God has manifested himself as an identity. And so we speak of the personhood of God.

The principle and the person of Father is someone we can identify. Moses goes up on the mountain of Sinai. He communes with the person of Sanat Kumara, the manifestation of the I AM THAT I AM, which is the Word itself.

The archangels who appeared to biblical figures, to Mother Mary, came in the personhood of God. They looked like people. They dressed in a certain fashion (not necessarily like people). Sometimes they so resembled people that they were described as "a man," or as "the two men in white" who came to attend Jesus' ascension.[3]

This shows that the manifestation of God as personhood is God manifesting himself in a relevancy for our own Path. And when God so manifests himself through an emissary of the Brotherhood, we deal with that person as though we were dealing with Brahma—Brahman in the beginning and Brahma as Father, as in the Trinity—Brahma, Vishnu and Shiva. We therefore take the representative of God as the manifestation of God because it is God's emissary, as Gabriel was God's messenger.[4]

The Rejection of One Son of God

Jesus made the statement, "Ye shall not see me henceforth, till ye shall say, Blessed is he that cometh in the name of the Lord."[5] This is when Jesus wept over Jerusalem, wept with an intensity, and expressed his longing to gather the children of Jerusalem to his heart. He cried out against the false hierarchy of the fallen ones who would not receive him and would not allow the little ones to receive him, and he prophesied the destruction of Jerusalem.

The messenger of God had come, his Son incarnate. He was rejected. And therefore he said, "You will not see me henceforth until you say, Blessed is he that cometh in the name of the Lord"—"I have come in the name of the Lord. You have rejected me. Therefore, you will not see the Christ again. You will not have access to the Son of God until you welcome the one who comes as my representative and in my name. In order to get to God, you must receive my representative, because you have rejected me, the Son of God."

And so it was a pronouncement of a judgment that the Christ would not appear to these fallen ones until they would welcome that Christ in the person of his messenger.

You may find yourself to be that very one who brings that test to someone, to anyone on earth. When you come in the name of the Lord and you are rejected because, supposedly, you have not had the theological training, you do not have the wisdom of the world, you are not dressed properly, you do not speak properly, or whatever imperfection may seem to be upon you, when there is the rejection of the representative of Truth, Truth therefore withdraws.

So you see the lie of the Protestant movement. It is a very frightening thing when you visit the cathedrals of Europe. You may go in one cathedral in Munich or in Nuremberg, a magnificent Catholic cathedral where there are tremendous statues of the saints, the Virgin, Christ, Saint Joseph, the archangels; you go into a Protestant cathedral that has been built since the Reformation—there is not one statue of anyone. It is barren, it is bare, and therefore, there is no Spirit of God within those churches either. The Spirit has gone out of them because the people have said, "I will only have God." And in rejecting his Son as the authority of judgment in their lives, in rejecting the hierarchy of angels who have not lost their first estate, they have actually rejected Almighty God. And these places are empty tombs.

Worse yet, go to London, England, to the most famous Protestant church there, Westminster Abbey. What do you find? It is not empty. There are *many* statues there, but what are they of? Kings and politicians. No saints are there. Now it is humans who have been exalted, or Nephilim gods who have been at the head of state. Here in a place of worship of Almighty God you find statues of men—men who have not been saints, who have not been pure, who have not been assumed into the body of Christ.

Therefore, by the rejection of Henry VIII of Catholicism

and the placing of himself as the authority of the Church, not only is there a devastation of the Church with no representative of the Godhead, but now the representatives of the Godhead are replaced. And many of these statues, I can tell you, are of embodied fallen angels and Watchers who have ruled in that government and in that nation.

A Vacuum Is Soon Filled with Other Identities

So you see, where there is a vacuum of the personages of God, of the saints and the ascended masters, by and by the vacuum is filled with those who have embodied the energy veil or evil. And so, we go from bad to worse.

You can see the very same thing if you go to the Polynesian cultures or the cultures of Central and South America, where you see images of gods, you see totem poles in Africa, you see images of something that is worshiped, knowing not quite what it is that they worship. But having some background in Sumer and the coming to the planetary body of the Nephilim gods,[6] you can see that these ancient cultures have been touched by them and that the depictions are so similar to the Sumerian tablets that one can understand that these peoples were taught to worship the Nephilim gods, the fallen ones in their spacecraft.

Again, a vacuum of the representation of the personages of God, of Sanat Kumara, Lord Maitreya—who surely were present and manifest in all the world in these ancient times, yet a nonalignment of the people with the Cosmic Christ. A vacuum allowed the Nephilim to come in and set up their totems, their statues, their focuses, and even their mechanical focuses anchoring the direct rays of the UFOs.

Understand, then, that if we do not have a love and devotion for the saints and the ascended masters, if we don't see ourselves as a part of the vast hierarchy of manifestation of God, ourselves occupying the office of chela, if we see ourselves alone in a universe, only accountable to an Almighty with whom we have very little rapport because he is so far away, that empty universe that we create, that barren consciousness of the pagan mind will soon be filled with other identities. Because the Nephilim always move in when we leave ourselves open.

Community Is Necessary

Therefore, the very concept of the community and communion of saints, which has been the tradition of Roman Catholicism, is necessary, not only because we rise and gain greater attainment and chelaship through the ascended masters, but also because they are occupying time and space with us. As Jesus said, "Occupy till I come."[7] The masters are occupying forcefields of light around us until the Christ come in us and is mature enough to neutralize the personages of evil—persons who have used free will to embody not the Trinity, not the Mother, but to embody the anti-Father, the anti-Christ, the anti-Son, the anti–Holy Spirit and the anti-Mother.

So it is one or the other. And this is, therefore, the foundation of our subject and our teaching.

The Dweller-on-the-Threshold:
The Enemy of the Light of the Christ in All

We have recently been given a tremendous decree by the Lord Jesus for the casting out of the dweller-on-the-threshold. And we have been taught that this dweller is the carnal mind, the nucleus of the anti-Self that we have created or that has been created by others, and that it is the dweller-on-the-threshold that is the enemy of the light of Christ in all people.

The teaching I bring you today is an understanding of a dweller-on-the-threshold that is a conglomerate carnal mind, representing a certain state of consciousness. For instance, we can name "the dweller-on-the-threshold that denies the communion of saints" or "the dweller-on-the-threshold that denies the embodiment of the personages of the Godhead."

In other words, there is a point of consciousness that is evil, that is the carnal mind, that is the not-self, and it is a collective consciousness fed by all people who have accepted the lie. It might represent a splinter, a section of many individuals' carnal mind or dweller-on-the-threshold, but all together it is a planetary momentum that is specifically the consciousness of denial of one thing—that denial being the denial of our communion with the ascended masters.

The Planetary Momentum, or Beast

You can talk about the dweller-on-the-threshold of marijuana, meaning the very core of its creation, the nucleus of the identity of the beast. When you see the word "beast" in the Book of Revelation, you understand that it is a conglomerate, a combination of many forces that have multiplied their momentum to move against the light. So we talk about planetary beasts. The word is also used in the divine sense where it is speaking about heavenly hierarchies. So in and of itself, it means a giant forcefield and form that has a consciousness, either of Almighty God as the four beasts that sit before the throne[8] or as of human creation.

We can speak about casting out the dweller-on-the-threshold of the war in Central America, the war in El Salvador, [or war in the Middle East]. We can name it and go after the beast or the dweller-on-the-threshold, which is that eye of the serpent just coming above the surface of the subconscious and wreaking havoc in Central America [or the Middle East].

We can talk about casting out the dweller-on-the-threshold of World Communism, the dweller-on-the-threshold of the Watchers and their godless creation. And we are dealing with a consciousness that over and over and over again, in the people who embody it, is the same thing. It's the very same vibration.

You could take a million people who are die-hard Communists today, and you could cast out the dweller-on-the-threshold of World Communism in those million people. And vibration for vibration, person by person, there would be no difference, because each one is embodying the same vibration. It's their vibration of their opinion about World Communism. It would not include the entire dweller-on-the-threshold of each person's consciousness. Some people have a greater momentum of human consciousness in this direction or in that direction.

It means cutting across the lines of force, the collective unconsciousness of a planet, and directing a decree into a specific lie, which because it is a lie and because some have believed it, they have given it life, it has gained an identity, gained a forcefield and has become a planetary momentum. This is where we start to go after very dangerous momentums that we see beginning to form upon the planet, exactly in that same way of pushing their heads above the surface so you just get a glimpse of them. And then they go under again.

The Flame of the Mother

I saw an interesting illustration of this concept as I happened to be looking out to sea a couple of days ago: all of a sudden there was a huge whale. You knew he was there by the giant spout of water. And then he dove under and there was a big tail. Then he swam some more and there were two spouts and two dives and two tails.

So we realize that in the great sea of light, in the great sea of God's consciousness, there is also a manifestation that holds the flame of the Mother. Appearing in the whale is always that point of the devotion of the Mother flame for the whole sea. It is like the whale is the Mother flame of a cosmic sea in elemental life. So we realize that those manifestations of God present themselves by showing a portion of themselves; a portion of their consciousness appears.

We understand what the apple tree is like when we pluck its fruit and taste it and we say, "This is the consciousness of the apple tree. This is the consciousness of the apple deva. This is the fruit it produces. Now I know what an apple tree is."

People will know you by the fruit that comes from your tree. And we know the world thought, and we know the presence of the dweller-on-the-threshold by an action, a manifestation that comes forth. We see it, we take a reading on it, and we go after it; and it penetrates deeper and deeper into the very depths of the sea until that dweller is bound.

Clearing the Personal Dweller

Most important for each one of us is the clearing of the personal dweller-on-the-threshold of the consciousness of the beast we are naming. In this case, the denial of the communion of saints is the point of the dweller in ourselves that we wish to be rid of and we are consciously casting out.

This may include any lurking doubt or fear that it is not possible for you to speak to the saints or for them to speak to you by the authorized means of the Holy Ghost through your

Christ Self under the direction of your I AM Presence; the sense that "No one can help me, I have this terrible problem, I have nowhere to go, no one to talk to, no one understands me, therefore, I'll just kill myself." That point of denial of the help of God and the communion of God is the absolute denial of the mighty archangels and hosts of the LORD who are there at any moment when we are in need.

Going after this state of consciousness is intended to clear us—beginning with this embodiment, and then all previous embodiments from the point of our beginning—of that particular lie of noncommunion and of rebellion or resentment or a sense of injustice against God that God himself, the Almighty, will not come down from his throne and deal with me and take care of this problem and kill my enemies and make me a glorious, victorious victor on the world scene, et cetera, and all these things that we imagine God should be doing for us.

God is not going to do that because God has sent his emissaries, and those emissaries will work with us within the framework of the Law itself. And the only enemy that any one of us has is the enemy within. It's the only enemy that can undo us. No enemy outside of ourselves can even touch or even have the authority to destroy us unless we give that enemy the authority to destroy us by our own fear of the enemy or our own hatred of the enemy, and so forth.

Understanding that that dweller is like a conglomerate within ourselves that has many facets—it's like a giant computer; it has many programs, much that we've put into it, much that we've accepted from the world—therefore we can go after it, for instance, by naming in each of the months of the year the personal and planetary dweller-on-the-threshold of the hierarchy of Aries, or of the other eleven signs.

We are in the sign of Aries. That which is anti-Aries, as

you know—conceit, deceit, arrogance and ego that manifests on that line—is a denial of our absolute Sonship and of the will of God and of the I AM Presence.

There are personality characteristics that are written up in astrology books that tell you about the temperament of an Aries person: the changeable quality, the impetuousness, the nonstability, misuse of power, misuse of sex, and so forth. There is a whole line of traits and characteristics that could be seen as the untransmuted Aries. And then there is a definition of the person of Aries as the person of Christ having the full attainment and power of that sign.[9]

It is a very joyous opportunity we have to realize that in each of the twelve lines of the clock, in our birth sign, our rising sign, sun sign, moon sign, and wherever we have planets, we have therefore an authority because we have a position astrologically to cast out the dweller-on-the-threshold of the entire momentum of misqualified energy of that planet or that system or that hierarchy.

Pulling Out the Dark Threads

This becomes a very joyous experience of pulling out the dark threads in the tapestry of our life, the tapestry of the Great Central Sun that is our divine identity, and it is the divine identity of our twin flame and of us together.

You all know that in the Royal Teton Retreat there is a great tapestry or painting of the twin flames who founded the retreat. Somewhere in cosmos in a retreat is a divine tapestry of you and your twin flame in all of the glory of your original creation standing in your fiery destiny with the authority of your lifestreams, and what it is your destiny to do for the evolutions of earth.

Therefore, there is a dweller-on-the-threshold of the anti-light of you and your twin flame. There's a dweller-on-the-threshold of the impostors of you and your twin flame—yourself in your positive and negative polarity.

Starting from that very beginning of prior golden ages when you had a much greater power than you have today, you can tackle the dweller-on-the-threshold that gradually, piece by piece, took from you the mighty light of Christ and inverted that light to create the beast.

Murder Is a Prominent Thoughtform on the World Scene

Now, I would like to give us one more thoughtform of the dweller-on-the-threshold that I think is extremely pertinent and apropos at this time. It is the consciousness—the planetary consciousness—of murder, assassination and the justification of war on the basis of the fact that the only way to solve an ideological problem is to eliminate the adversary or the opponent. In other words, if you destroy his flesh and blood, you destroy the idea. And of course, this is ludicrous—nothing could be further from the truth.

Murder is a very prominent thoughtform on the world scene today. And in fact, I have received any number of letters and notes from people telling me that they are having dreams in which they see someone holding a gun and firing a gun, either at the chelas or the messenger, at one another or at an unknown person.

The image of the gun itself being held and fired is a thoughtform that actually coalesces the hate and hate creation in the Dark Cycle that we are winding up, the Dark Cycle of Aquarius, where planetary momentums of hatred of the light are reaching a fever pitch in this last six-week cycle of the year, moving toward April 23, when we will come into the two o'clock line, which itself is a momentum of death. On that line we will be dealing with that momentum of the Pisces anti-light: fear, doubt, human questioning and records of death. It's like the death of Pisces casting its shadow before it comes, combining with the last vestiges of the hate and hate creation against the light of Saint Germain on the one o'clock line.[10]

It's wonderful that we have the Law and the teaching to understand and to be able to interpret the acceleration and the agitation of the astral plane that many people have sensed.

It Is Impossible to Kill the Christ

Now, I would like you to look at the philosophy of murder as a means to solve problems. It's used by the Mafia, it's used in war, it's used when people want to get money for drugs and they have to kill those from whom they're robbing, and it's also a thoughtform of suicide.

First of all, Jesus proved that murder does not work. They murdered him, but he never died. They crucified him, he was resurrected, and by the very process of the victory over Death and Hell, he multiplied his Christ Self, his Christ body, and he sprang up as a lily in the garden of our hearts. Jesus Christ lives forevermore in the heart of every one of his lovers, his disciples, his followers.

So the attempt to put out the light of the Son of God only results in the absolute multiplication of that one. It is impossible to kill the Christ. And the flesh and blood is not the identity of the person, but only its house.

Those who murder the house determine that effectively they will stop the action, the fiery destiny, the soul purpose of that one, and thereby slow down their divine purpose on earth. The continuity of consciousness is apparent right where you sit. You have lived before. You have died before. Most of you at one time or another have fallen on a battlefield of life, killed by the enemy in a war or in a murder or in an assassination. And yet, you sit here alive and well, in full faculties and consciousness with your I AM Presence and Christ Self.

The whole sad routine has resulted in nothing but a delay and a postponement of the ultimate confrontation, which is the casting out of the dweller-on-the-threshold. Because that is the point that must be bound, and it can only be removed or killed through transmutation—it can't be killed with a bullet or a gun or any form of murder—the dweller will live on.

On the other hand, an additional proof that murder doesn't work is that if you kill the evil man, that one will lose his body, go off into the astral plane raging with anger and revenge, combine with astral entities, demons, conglomerates of forcefields, and move against the lightbearers, move against those who destroyed him in a vendetta, and reembody with that consciousness of revenge.

By and by, when the evil one becomes a black magician, he has learned the power of dispersion. Dispersion is the opposite feat to multiplying one's light body and living forevermore in the heart of the disciple. Dispersion is the dispersing of the soul into many, many particles—even thousands of particles—and depositing those particles in people whom you, therefore, as a black magician, wish to control.

Therefore, if you have in the dweller-on-the-threshold in your subconscious a momentum of, let's say, resentment, you might very well be the unconscious recipient of a larger momentum of resentment of the Evil One or the black magicians of the planet and find yourself the unwitting tool one day of an expression of resentment that astounds you. And you say to yourself, "I cannot understand what came over me or how I could possibly have so expressed myself or acted in this manner, because I surely do not have this resentment."

Perhaps you do not have it, but you might have had a grain of it in your own carnal mind, and in an unguarded moment—an uneducated, undisciplined moment—you may have been an open door for a larger momentum of resentment. And therefore, you reap the karma of a planetary momentum of resentment focused through you through such an evil one.

Not All at Once, but Day by Day

This is why we are so grateful to have our tube of light and the calls to Archangel Michael to protect us even from ourselves while we are in the process of working out our salvation in the laboratory of the soul. We cannot get rid of this carnal mind all at once, but at least it can be sealed, it can be capped, and not become a liability and a point of vulnerability within us to preying forces—we know not what. This is why we decree on a daily basis, because sometimes planetary momentums are very agitating, they bring in tremendous riptides, and if we let ourselves become wide open to such forces, all of a sudden, we find ourselves out of control.

When you experience such a state in your life and you have tremendous remorse for it, you should not necessarily think that it happened because you have little attainment. It may have happened because you actually have a great light around you through your service, your association with the Brotherhood and your decrees, and you came under an extraordinary attack. And for one reason or another, you let yourself be split or divided and therefore lose control.

So, it is a measure of understanding the adversary, the impostor of your chelaship, and a realization, of course, that the energy coming against you is vicious and that you must have a superior guard against a moment of self-indulgence or a moment of neglect and being off guard and therefore allowing yourself to tie in to a flood of darkness.

The Lashback—Understanding the Adversary

When you give these calls on the dweller—whether you're tackling a planetary momentum or one specific individual—you find that within an hour, two hours, three hours or six hours or a half a day, you may notice a lashback, where that particular momentum of the dweller has become angry because in the process of casting out the dweller, you have awakened it. You wake the sleeping serpent when you go after the dweller.

How is this so? We'll take the first lie we dealt with today—the lie of the denial of communion with the saints of God and rebellion against hierarchy and rebellion against the Most High God. That dweller may be lurking in the subconscious of vast numbers of people, but they may not be conscious of it; it has not reached their conscious mind, they have not acted upon it.

For instance, every Protestant in America and the world is not walking around aggressively denying the communion of saints. He just doesn't happen to be partaking of it because no one told him it was his right or his authority. He's not thinking about it, but it is programmed into him. And when you deal with the dweller of that particular situation, it's going to arouse that dweller wherever it is.

There's nothing wrong with that. This is what happens in the last days; this is what happens in the final judgment of God. People's sins have to be exposed, and that's the reason Christ comes into the world. Your Christ Self comes into manifestation for judgment, as Jesus said: "For judgment I am come into this world."[11]

When the Christ consciousness hits your chakras and your four lower bodies, you're going to be made a little bit uncomfortable and see things you didn't see before and have to make some fast choices and fast decisions: "By the way, whose side am I on? Am I on the side of this old human creation or am I on the side of this greater light, even though I'm uncomfortable in this light?"

The Creation of Mechanization Man

Now getting back to the point of why murder doesn't work: In the case of the Evil One, it's the same thing. The Evil One is not his flesh and blood either. The Evil One is a state of consciousness. So the flesh-and-blood body is murdered, as the Mafia kill people all the time, but they go floating in the astral plane. Karmic ties are made. Those individuals aggressively reincarnate, perhaps in the families of the very ones who killed them, and that consciousness will still have to be dealt with. Ultimately and finally, the victim and the murderer will have to deal with the opposing consciousness.

Then you have this ability of dispersion of the black magician and the additional ability, when you get to the Nephilim gods—since their coming to the planet in ancient times, from a half a million years ago, prior to that and since then—of their creation of mechanization man. Into mechanization man, the Nephilim placed their genes. In combination with *Homo erectus,* they created a new type of body, a new type of individual.

So, in every one of those created bodies of mechanization man will be the record of their dweller-on-the-threshold and their carnal mind, their momentum, their identity. And this they know, and this is why they have created life.

God created you and me and our body temples to have a point of devotion and a point of love and a point of communion and a point where God, through your Christ consciousness, evolves and the universe and the cosmic consciousness of Christ gets bigger, because each one of us evolves the flame of love. The Nephilim create mechanization man in order to have a focus to hate. God creates sons to love; Nephilim create mechanization man as a focus to hate.

If you can create a million mechanization-man forcefields on the planet, get them to propagate and multiply, then, when you as a Nephilim want to embody and run for office, you can rally your million mechanization men around you because they're just like you, because you're inside of them. So they're your puppets. You've got them not only brainwashed, you've got them gene-washed. Their genes are just like yours. So you get them fighting for you, decreeing for you, working for you and being your slaves, because you are their god. They worship you because they have no other creator. They don't believe in Almighty God because you don't believe in Almighty God.

This is the philosophy of the Nephilim. They say, "I am immortal, not because I am willing to submit to the LORD God Almighty, no. I am immortal because I have placed myself inside of my creation. Just like you, God. You see, God, you've got nothing on me. I can do anything you can do, and I can do it better." That's the line of the Nephilim gods.

And so, not only do they put their genes in mechanization man, but they clone themselves, making exact carbon copies. If you are going after the Nephilim consciousness of the planet or a particular individual whom you happen to know is the embodiment of a Nephilim, you have to name it as close as you can get to it. If you want to close in on a particular consciousness of Nephilim, you can say, "all Nephilim embodying in the I AM Race" or "all Nephilim embodying in the United States of America." And then you have to say, "and all mechanization man, clones, carbon copies and lifestreams in whom there is an implant of the carnal mind of the dweller-on-the-threshold and the genes of that one."

The Fallacy of War—Nothing Is Solved

When you come down to it, you see, therefore, that it is not murder that eliminates the enemy, but it is transmutation. And there is no point lining up people on a battlefield, killing each other off—brother against brother—to solve a problem of ideology. If they're all dead and they're all drenched in blood and the civilization is destroyed, the two opposing ideas will remain. They will be there after the whole war is over.

We won World War II, but Korea followed after. We have the Middle East, we've got a buildup of nuclear weapons, and everybody fears war again. And all over the world, death is used as an instrument of revenge, of hatred, of making people pay the price. Nothing is solved; the hatred remains.

There has been bloodshed, but the consciousness of those people lives on; it will reincarnate. Arabs will embody among Jews, Jews will embody among Arabs; they will invert their hatreds. A Jew that dies on the battlefield gets born to an Arab; he carries the same momentum of hatred, but he's taught from childhood, now he hates the Jews. Now he's an Arab. Now he says, "I'm an Arab, I hate Jews." So he goes and kills Jews, and he flips over and the next embodiment he's a Jew. "Oh, now I'm a Jew, now I hate Arabs." But the hatred lives on. The hatred lives on.

If you take a spirit of planetary fanaticism, it lives on. A fanatical Communist can reembody as a fanatical right-winger in some South American country, and the hatred moves right on. It has another point of fixation, but no problem is solved. This is the state of the planet Earth, this is where we are.

Delivering the Planet of a State of Consciousness

Our beloved Lord and master and friend and brother Jesus Christ has given us the call for the casting out of the dweller and the Judgment Call because he wants us to deliver the planet of a state of consciousness. This is not the elimination of flesh and blood. This is not a call that justifies divine or cosmic murder—not in the least. It is a judgment of a state of consciousness that is focalized and represented by a certain individual, for which he must receive now the karmic accountability and understand the unreality of that state by having a level of judgment delivered to his doorstep.

We receive these judgments, great and small, daily as we learn from our mistakes. And so, day by day as we go through life, we learn what part of our unreal self, our dweller, we are through with. We want nothing more to do with that unreal self. We go through an experience, we've had it, it's the last time we're going to indulge that particular momentum; we go after it and we say, "I cast out the dweller-on-the-threshold of my consciousness of impatience, of anger, of envy, of anxiety" —whatever state you want to name.

You see, God cannot simply take a sledgehammer to your carnal mind or my carnal mind—with one fell swoop we give the call and, all of a sudden, the dweller is gone. The process of Christhood is an evolutionary process. We have to consent, by the seat of the conscious mind, that we are doing away with a point of unreality in ourselves. And therefore, we have to live on earth and be able to observe ourselves as in a laboratory. We observe our momentums and we say, "I don't like that momentum," but it happens again and again. And we realize it's an adversary, it's a momentum that threatens to take over our body temple; from time to time it takes over our mind.

And so we say, "That is not the light, that is not my Christhood, that's not my Real Self, that's not who I want to be; I cast it out." And that's when you get into the core of your Christhood with this absolute one-pointedness of soul, mind and heart and you say, "I am casting it out." And because you have such a will and a determination that you put into your decree and such an illumination of what it is you're dealing with, it is cast out.

Fierceness and Determination to Cast Out
the Dweller-on-the-Threshold

The miracle and the absolute fiat will manifest if you have the determination. So this, above all decrees, is a decree into which you have to insert your highest Christ consciousness, your highest awareness. It's not a decree you can just recite. It's the instrument of the Christ casting out the money-changers in the temple.[12] He was fierce, he was determined, he yelled at them, he denounced them, he rebuked them. And that's what you must do. That's what you do with that point of the entity, that point of the demon in your own world. And only then will it work. It starts getting not to work when you just recite it mechanically.

Now you can get just as fierce and determined about the planetary dweller-on-the-threshold of marijuana: "As I live, Almighty God, I will not tolerate this beast on the planet. I will stand in the earth in my I AM Presence. And if it's the only thing I do in this embodiment, I am determined to cast out the dweller-on-the-threshold of marijuana."

You go after any of its consciousness in your own world—sloth, passivity, noncaring, illusion, floating off into other planes and dreaming and reverie. Whatever the chemical marijuana does to the state of mind of a person, if you yourself see in yourself those same types of tendencies—even though you may have never smoked marijuana or it has been many years since you have taken it—a portion of that planetary dweller has seeped its way into you unaware. Procrastination, passivism—these are part of the qualities of the marijuana dweller-on-the-threshold.

So the more you can diagnose and define the dweller that you're working on in the world, the more you can see that, in order to conquer it, you have to get it out of your own being.

Those who make their life's calling this determination to wage a war on marijuana—who become very familiar with it, read all the books on it, attend lectures on it, do counseling with young people who take it—get a very intimate knowledge of that beast. And therefore, when you make your call, you have an authority that people who are totally ignorant do not have. You have an authority of the seat of your conscious mind, one with your Christ Self, that now can identify this beast as though you had actually dissected it in a laboratory. You can name every part of it, and you can go after it.

When you start doing that and you start dedicating your life to that particular call, you will get the whole planetary momentum of a backlash against you. From whom? The pushers, the growers, the Mafia, everybody who benefits from the marijuana beast and everybody who's enslaved by it, all of their carnal mind will be a backlash on you when you make that call.

172 | THE ENEMY WITHIN

The Reinforcement of Community

This is the great force of our community, where we gather for a weekend seminar and we say we're going to give our total attention to this subject and decree on it. We're one group, we're many, many thousand strong, we're all over the planet. On this specific weekend we're working on this specific subject, and this marathon and this hearing of lectures brings together a focalization.

The backlash comes, but we're in our sanctuary; we're one mind, one heart, one group of decreers. And as the backlash comes, we're still decreeing. And so it gets beaten again and again. And the calls to Archangel Michael give protection as well as the authority to the hosts of the LORD to bind it. This is why we've had so many successes, because of the vast momentum of our community worldwide and our concentration.

Sometimes when you stand in an isolated spot and make a call on something so horrendous, you'll feel a trembling and a backlash because of the nonreinforcement of community. And the reinforcement of community, as we know it, is also the reinforcement of the communion of the saints.

So we need our community on earth, we need our land, we need our ranch, we need that concentrated forcefield, and we need the Great White Brotherhood in heaven. And when we have communion with the saints and communion with the saints here below on earth, we have the indomitable power of Almighty God to win.

The Core of World Hatred

Now getting back to this principle of murder as the means to fight the enemy or destroy and get ahead with whatever we are dealing with, the fallacy is great. And therefore, we must go to the core of this thoughtform of the gun—the gun being fired. The core of it is world hatred.

If hatred is allowed to fester in the human soul or in any of the chakras or the four lower bodies, it reaches a momentum where the person's hatred forces him to draw the conclusion: "The only way out of this dilemma of me and the person I hate so much is for that person to cease to exist. I wish he were dead. I wish she was dead. She ought to be dead. Maybe I ought to see to it that she or he is dead," because one cannot live with the hatred, because it eats one alive. Hatred is an immense disease.

We're sitting in the middle of planetary momentums of hatred. And the thoughtform of it is, "Kill the enemy"— whoever anybody perceives as the enemy.

There's been a lot of talk about guns in the past five years—the idea that we should restrict guns, have gun laws, deprive people of the right to bear arms, interfere with the Constitution. The way to get rid of murder is to have everybody not have guns.

Well, what happens when they don't have guns? They start using knives. They start using other weapons, because it didn't destroy the hatred. If we destroy all guns, we're going to destroy murder? No. That's just as fallacious as saying, "If we kill everybody, we're going to win the war," because the gun is not the hatred either. It's an instrument, just like the body is an instrument of a state of consciousness.

When we see a thoughtform and when we have dreams of this nature, it is the angels giving us the understanding that there is a fever pitch of world hatred mounting, and because we are alchemists of the sacred fire, we are here to make the call. And that's the sum and substance of what you see and what you feel. You should never be threatened or allow yourself to be engaged in anxiety by such thoughtforms or dreams. You should see that they are prophetic only of what you need to come into the sanctuary and decree about, and that it is unreal.

Unreality is ferocious, it's fierce, and it presents itself as a tremendous manifestation appearing to be Real. No matter how large error is or how vicious, it is still not real. Whether it's a bug that you swat or whether it's World Communism, it's still the same personality of evil. And you have to overcome your fear of the bug and your fear of World Communism. And when you do, no manifestation of evil can tempt you to engage in a fear of the thoughtform of the gun or to now see that gun in your hand as the means to end it all, either ending your life or ending the life of someone who is somehow bothering you.

You must know that the entire planetary momentum of war and murder that's been going on for millions of years fears the voice of one son of God who punctures its lie and declares that it shall no longer be.

The Carnal Mind, or Serpent

The using of this call for the casting out of the dweller-on-the-threshold is an immense power to impel you toward your ascension and to new levels of attainment on the Path, because it is so specific in the binding of the momentum of the carnal mind.

This carnal mind takes the form of the serpent within the electronic belt, beginning as a nucleus of the egg of the serpent, the initial seed idea, and building itself until in its final full-grown form, it is like a dinosaur or a dragon that we read about in the Book of Revelation. From the Serpent in the Garden to the dragon of Revelation, we see through the Bible the planetary evolution of evil; even as we see, through the consciousness of the patriarchs, the planetary evolution of the

Christ. Both histories are traced. It's all there.

Now, we also have another energy within us that is the coiled serpent, the Goddess Kundalini, in the base-of-the-spine chakra, which contains that sealed energy of the coiled serpent, as it is called. And even when this energy rises as the Kundalini on the spine and is fixed at the third eye, it is shown in the caduceus symbol as a serpent with its head at this point, showing that the Kundalini has an identity and a consciousness. The similarity of the thoughtform tells us that the building of the dweller-on-the-threshold is a direct perversion of the Goddess Kundalini, the sacred force of life.

People siphon off the base-of-the-spine chakra energies. And when they become black magicians, they specifically know how to raise that Kundalini and use it to promote and propagate evil. This is what the fallen ones did when the Watchers and the Nephilim created mechanization man. They were creating it out of their own life-force, propagating a species of the ani-mal or the animated evil.

Reclaiming the Light of the Kundalini

Therefore, we understand that as we withdraw the light of the dweller-on-the-threshold, we should be returning the light of the Kundalini. The fire of the spine should increase, because we are reclaiming the light of the Mother flame, which you also know is the flame of the ascension.

It stands to reason that in the process of slaying the dweller, we will be coming up against the challenges and the temptations of world momentums of the misuse of this life-force.

We often associate with the misuse of the base-of-the-spine chakra the misuse of sex. But it is not sex alone. War itself is a misuse of the base chakra; aggression, hatred, great intensities of darkness come out of that chakra.

However, there is a very definite level where the reclaiming of the light of the Kundalini does involve the temptation of sexuality that comes from the Serpent himself or the fallen ones, which is the temptation to use that life-force for the purposes of sensuality and sense gratification, for the purposes of outer glamour of the person, for that sexual pride, and that figure that is associated with the virile type of male or the cunning female.

There is the ordinate and correct use of the life-force that has to do with the procreation of life and the exchange of the love of all of the chakras of being with the twin flame or with one with whom one is lawfully joined in marriage. Those who are initiates on the Path obviously have a tremendous respect for the life-force and for its use and do not squander the energy and do not misuse it.

The temptation is to believe that because Serpent has undone and misused the Kundalini fire and engaged and drawn the people of the planet into wholesale sex, illicit sex, perverted sex, homosexuality, that, therefore, all sex is bad and evil and any and all sex, therefore, comes from the sinister force.

What we have to understand is that there is a very definite line drawn and that the life-force, when it is raised on the spinal altar and when it blossoms in the chakras and gives forth the fruit of the crown, creates the identity and the personality of the individual. That individual, therefore, manifesting the totality of life, becomes a being able to give and receive in the same levels and the same chakras with the twin flame or with one who is joined in marriage.

People are referred to as being sexual beings or sexual animals. The fact is that we are beings of the life-force and of the sacred fire. It rises upon the spine; it seals the identity of the chakras. That is the Mother flame. The light of the Father descends from the I AM Presence and the Christ Self, and the threefold flame in the heart expands.

Without the life-force of the Kundalini being raised, we do not have the complement to the light of the threefold flame to hold the balance in the temple. When you have the descent of God and the ascent of God within you, you have a complete and closed circuit of Alpha and Omega, and therefore, your chakras can emit both qualities and manifestations.

Now, at the point when you are reclaiming the light wrongly vested in the dweller, you will be reclaiming a large momentum of the white fire of the base chakra. It's the ascension flame. It's the Goddess Kundalini. It's the power with which you weave the Deathless Solar Body.

At the moment that light is active in your temple, it creates the original power of attraction whereby the Watchers and the fallen ones came down to the daughters of men and took themselves wives.[13] Those who have a greater amount of light in the aura are always seen by the fallen ones as those whom they desire to have, sexually. So the more light you have in your body, the more protection you need.

You need the protection also through illumination, by way of understanding that until all the momentums of the misuse of the base chakra are also transmuted in our own subconscious, we may momentarily become vulnerable to the illusions of those outside of us—of Serpent and his seed, et cetera—of a male-female attraction that is not an attraction of the heart or of the I AM Presence or of the Christ or one of attainment. It is energies used over and over again that are dwelling in the subconscious

These energies are there, and they come up for transmutation. But instead of being transmuted, because there is desire lurking in the subconscious to find the ultimate relationship, the ultimate attraction, the ultimate union, the individual does not proceed with caution, but leaps into the idea, "This must be this fantastic relationship, this must be what I've been waiting for for centuries." And to do that, of course, is to jump into the pot of one's own illusion and one's own fantasy.

Sex Is the Great Illusion

One has to be very guarded, because you are dealing, we all are dealing, with cosmic energies and light with which we are not entirely familiar. We don't understand the ramifications of what light does in our four lower bodies and how it does activate unreality. When the unreality comes to the surface, we must be very vigilant. And so it is wise to move to cast out the dweller-on-the-threshold within one's own subconscious of the illusions of astrology concerning the misuse of the sacred fire and polarities and attractions that are definitely of the human animal and of the serpent type.

There is often a rationalization by those who have a very strong conscious will who will say, "Now, this attraction has nothing to do with sex; it's only a great lofty thing of the heart, and therefore, it must be real." That is not necessarily so, because it is very easy to take the Kundalini that does root in a misqualified use of sex, raise it to the heart, experience this energy through the heart, and say, "OK, this thing is of my heart and of my higher consciousness, so it must be right." We must not hop to those conclusions, because they are not necessarily correct.

There is no greater illusion on this planetary body than sex, except death itself. Sex is the great delusion and illusion, and of course, its counterpart is death, because the squandering of the base chakra is death. People have squandered it so long that their lives are shortened; they get into disease and old age, decay and death very quickly compared to other ages and other experiences.

So we realize that in the human animal—which we declare to be ourselves no part of, yet which we have the remnant of in the momentum of the four lower bodies—as Mark Prophet has said in one of his lectures, "From the moment you're born, you're dying." In the human consciousness, the moment you begin to live, you begin to die, and all acts actually lead to the final act of so-called death.

The Path Can Be Treacherous

This is why in holy orders there is a certain propriety of order and standards set forth for the interaction of men and women. It is because it is known by the Brotherhood that in all that you do, in all of your decrees, you are transmuting misuses of the chakras. And we begin with the base chakra when we deal with life itself, even as it is the life of the heart and the threefold flame.

Therefore, in the process of transmutation, we are all in a state of flux. We have not arrived to the perfect Self and its identification and its strength in Christ. And yet, we have decided to leave the old man or the old woman with the old vibrations.

This path can be a treacherous one. And it is a time of great vulnerability. It is a time of swift changes, where the person you were yesterday is not the person you are today. And the same is true for everyone else. So it's important that we discover who we are and who someone else is before we decide to draw up a contract of a lifelong, legal situation of marriage, or even business partnerships.

As you walk this path, you will feel gradually and not by

force a greater and greater strength coming in the spine, coming at the back of the neck, coming at the head and the crown, the more you pursue the great joyous discipline of the Path. And you will feel this great power, increment by increment, because it is directed by your I AM Presence and Christ Self.

We do no such thing as tantric yoga or any other practices to force the raising of the Kundalini. It rises naturally as we purify our four lower bodies and as we have the strength to maintain and sustain it, to guard it, and to not have violent actions happen in our temple that can cause anger or insanity or distress. (This has been known to occur when people raise the Kundalini prematurely.) That is why the masters sometimes wait many, many years for their chelas before that fire begins to rise. This is why we give calls to Archangel Michael and the violet flame.

The goal of the Path is for this Kundalini to be raised in you, and it should not be rushed, it can't be rushed; and you should understand that if your body is quiescent and you do not feel this light, it is entirely in order. God is protecting you and allowing you to build a momentum of stability and balance in your threefold flame. The threefold-flame balance corresponds with the three parts of this Kundalini—the *ida,* the *pingala* and the *sushumna,* which is the central canal of its flow.

The carnal mind is very subtle. And since the ego is used to reinforcing itself sexually—people like to know that they are sexually attractive, that others find them attractive—there are all kinds of subtle ways that people convey this: through conversation, through the way they wear their clothes, the way they walk, thoughts they think, and so forth.

And if you find yourself so smitten with a member of the opposite sex that you have more attention flowing to that person than you have flowing to your I AM Presence, then at that point, you have lost a point of attainment. And that is not the nature of true love. You can be in love, you can love someone, you can be married and have absolute devotion to that person, and yet your mind is stayed on God. God is first, last and always in the relationship, and the relationship is free, buoyant, joyous, and it does not have the burdens of the intensity of these types of hooks and matrices.

Mastery of the Life-Force

These are things you need to know, because you know that the path of the East, as well as the path of Jesus, was a mastery of the sexual energies, a mastery of the life-force and a mastery of the Kundalini. The path of that mastery in the Aquarian age includes, as you know, celibacy as well as the path of the family and the path of raising children.

The same principle is present as we were just discussing in the concept of murder itself. Murder is no means to an end. It accomplishes nothing; it does not remove opposing forces. So it is also true that marriage or the use of sex itself does not necessarily deprive you of the mastery of the Kundalini or the life-force—but it may; it depends on the mastery that you bring to the endeavor, to the subject, to the love and to being a family.

People can be unmarried and walking the celibate path and continually misqualifying and squandering the Kundalini fire because of impurity of consciousness. People can be married and wholly the guardians of this life-force in one another. In fact, the highest purpose of marriage is for two people to be the guardians of the Kundalini fire and the threefold flame within one another. They create together the circle of oneness, the locking of their energy, so that both are protected from the entire world momentum of the Serpent's version of sex and human sexuality.

The community itself is intended to be a protection to all its members from the problems that remain unresolved because the Kundalini is not raised. The teachings of the sacred fire breath and Djwal Kul's meditation,[14] a healthy but not over-rich diet, basic exercise and yoga postures will assist all of you, whether married or single, in having greater attainment of the life-force.

The days are being shortened for the elect, which means the days of your own mastery of your Kundalini are being shortened also. And you will be amazed at how much attainment you will have by just having the freedom of a little bit of illumination and a little bit of a correction of your own consciousness. We do not have to be the victims of our own self-imposed guilt or frustration merely because of the ignorance of techniques of the spirit and of the physical body.

The Teachings of Lord Himalaya

I would like to tell you that this teaching has come forth from that sacred-fire essence transferred to my heart from beloved Lord Himalaya. As you pursue the path of deep meditation on one or more of the ascended masters, you will find that the teaching of that one will blossom in your heart as a lily. It will be the lily of the Kundalini fire of that master, the lily of your own raised life-force, the lily of your resurrected Christ Presence, all converging in the heart.

I would like you to know that it is the tradition of Lord Himalaya that he does not speak to his disciples, but they meditate before him and must perceive his thoughtforms by an intense attunement with his mind. Obviously, we have had dictations from Lord Himalaya as he has directed, through his

Christ consciousness, instruction for us.

Today, he gave it in this manner so that you could see the impartation of his mind to my own and its delivery to all of us at our level of understanding. This is eternal, immortal teaching. It is stepped down by Himalaya and stepped down by my own office and your own Christ Self for us to derive the greatest benefit.

I am profoundly grateful for this instruction, and I bow before the blue-lotus flame of Himalaya and of your own hearts, the budding blue lotus, and of my own and of every ascended master.

You can close your eyes and visualize every saint and cosmic being holding the thoughtform of the blue gentian or the blue lotus, a fiery, deep sapphire blue flower of the heart. You can see through that point of visualization the oneness of all cosmos and of the entire Great White Brotherhood.

How joyous it is to be free, free from the dweller-on-the-threshold in every form and mode, and to know that not any manifestation of it at all, in this or any world whatsoever, shall ever again threaten or cause to fear or tremble the sons of God. For God has given us the key, and God has given us the Presence of the Lord Jesus Christ with us to reinforce our attainment and light and fearlessness flame.

CHAPTER NINE

Filling the Vacuum

The Editors

As we have seen, the binding and casting out of the dweller-on-the-threshold is a key element of the spiritual path. However, as we have also seen, it is not the totality of the Path. For at the same time as we are denying the dweller and its various manifestations, we must also be putting on the consciousness of the Christ Self and the elements of the Christ consciousness.

This is a step-by-step process. Day by day, increment by increment, the dweller can be reduced in size and we can become more of our Christ Self, and these two elements of the Path do need to go hand in hand. For if all our house is filled with the dweller, we are not making room for the Christ to enter. And just as importantly, when we cast out the dweller, we must fill the vacuum.

Therefore, when we cast out the personal dweller-on-the-threshold, we must invite the Christ Self to enter into our being. As we remove the manifestations of the dweller—pride, anger, rebellion, or whatever they might be—we must incorporate into our life the corresponding qualities of the Christ consciousness.

This is not an overnight process. We can't simply stamp out all vestiges of negativity in our being in one action. These things are intertwined with our positive momentums, and this conglomerate makes up our current identity and provides the platform for our life and our service. Jesus explained this principle in the parable of the tares and the wheat:

> Another parable put he forth unto them, saying, The kingdom of heaven is likened unto a man which sowed good seed in his field: but while men slept, his enemy came and sowed tares among the wheat, and went his way. But when the blade was sprung up, and brought forth fruit, then appeared the tares also.
>
> So the servants of the householder came and said unto him, Sir, didst not thou sow good seed in thy field? from whence then hath it tares? He said unto them, An enemy hath done this.
>
> The servants said unto him, Wilt thou then that we go and gather them up? But he said, Nay; lest while ye gather up the tares, ye root up also the wheat with them. Let both grow together until the harvest: and in the time of harvest I will say to the reapers, Gather ye together first the tares, and bind them in bundles to burn them: but gather the wheat into my barn.[1]

We find the tares and the wheat growing together in our own consciousness. We cannot simply uproot the whole of the dweller all at once—we would lose the platform of our evolution. But we can day by day decide to care for the good wheat of the Christ consciousness and no longer feed the dweller. In this way we can prepare for the time of the final harvest, the point on the Path when the dweller can be removed entirely. In the meantime, we can keep the dweller bound and in check and work to develop the qualities of

Christhood in our lives.

One flame that it is necessary for us to embody is the flame of peace. As long as we are caught between the Christ and the Dweller, there will be the warring in the members that Paul spoke of.[2] If we do not keep the dweller bound and in check, there is that warring, that tug-of-war between the two forces—like the cartoons you see of a person with a little angel whispering in one ear and a little demon whispering in the other. This warring in our members can be replaced by the flame of peace.

The quality of peace is often misunderstood. People interpret peace to be pacifism or passivity, whereas the true flame of peace is a dynamic and active energy. Jesus was the Prince of Peace, the great master of the sixth dispensation and the sixth ray of peace; he demonstrated the many shadings of the flame of peace in different episodes of his life. For example, it was only through casting out the moneychangers that the flame of peace could be brought to the temple of Jerusalem. Jesus' peace was not a namby-pamby, wishy-washy sentimentality; he had a strength and a presence that could galvanize people and change a world.

This is what we need to have. When we establish the flame of peace within ourselves, we can then widen our boundaries and our sphere of spiritual responsibility. In ever-widening circles of responsibility, we can bring peace to ourselves, to our families, to our communities, and then to the world.

This is how the world is changed—at the point of individual accountability.

The final chapter of this book is a lecture by Elizabeth Clare Prophet that outlines principles for developing this quality of peace in our lives. These principles have been drawn from teachings delivered by the Elohim Peace and Aloha. Among their teachings are found ten specific keys to help us develop the quality of peace.

CHAPTER TEN

Ten Keys for Finding Peace Within

Elizabeth Clare Prophet

The Elohim Peace and Aloha have admonished us that "the warring in the members must be cast into the sacred fire, no matter what the cost.... Pay the price, whatever it takes, to give up that indulgence of discord. For each time you allow it, it becomes bigger and bigger. It becomes one with the dweller-on-the-threshold until you are crying out for saviours, such as the archangels or the Elohim, to deliver you. And yet you have created the entire scene; you have created the schism in yourself. Who else can do it but you? You must cast out that dragon."[1]

The Elohim Peace and his complement, Aloha, are the Elohim of the sixth ray. This is the purple and gold ray of peace, brotherhood, ministration and service. Elohim is a plural noun translated as "God" in the Bible. In Genesis 1:26, God (Elohim) said, "Let us make man in our image, after our likeness." Elohim refers to the Alpha, the Omega, the yin-yang polarity, so this Godhead is the "Divine Us."

From their retreat, the Temple of Peace over the Hawaiian Islands, they focus the energies of the solar-plexus chakra of the planet and radiate ribbons of Cosmic Christ Peace over the entire earth. Souls who are to embody the sixth-ray virtues of peace, ministration and service on behalf of all life study for a time at the Temple of Peace in preparation for their mission. So if you haven't been to the Hawaiian Islands physically, you can definitely be there at night studying under the Elohim Peace and Aloha in their retreat.

The Solar Plexus, the Place of Peace

The solar plexus is the chakra of the sixth ray and the opening for the release of peace, and from it should flow ribbons of Cosmic Christ Peace. But more often than not, people engage in anti-peace.

The Elohim Peace and Aloha teach us how to put up a shield over our solar plexus to protect ourselves from receiving the anger and the burdens and the discord that daily come our way. That kind of discord comes through radio and TV. And it comes through the droning on throughout the planetary body of anger, of people's dissatisfaction with their lot, their rejection of their karma, their rejection of God, and their refusal to make their peace with God and to balance the wrongs they have committed.

Raise the Sacred Fire to the Upper Chakras

The solar-plexus chakra is the first chakra below the heart. When we are in the Christ consciousness and in the Christ mind, we maintain the vigil of the fire of God that is given to us from our I AM Presence from the level of our Holy Christ Self through our heart chakra.

So the heart chakra, the secret chamber of the heart, the throat chakra, the third eye and the crown are where we need to be in consciousness. This does not mean that we cut off the energies of the lower chakras. It means that we raise the

The Seven Chakras

sacred fire from the base-of-the-spine chakra sufficiently to nourish the functions of the body.

The raised sacred fire is the rising of the Kundalini. It rises to the place of the third eye and can be sustained there unless we choose to direct the full fire of our being through the heart, in invocations, or through the throat chakra. Or we may desire to anchor that energy of the sacred fire in the secret chamber of the heart, where we commune with the Christ and we commune with Gautama Buddha.

If we desire to focus entirely through the third eye for vision, for direction, then that is where we will place the sacred fire. If we desire to engage in profound meditation in the octaves of light with Buddhas and Bodhisattvas, Sanat Kumara or the Cosmic Christ, we will have our focus at the crown.

When you raise the sacred fire of the Kundalini from the base chakra and that fire meets the descending fire of God in your heart chakra, then you have the balance of the Alpha and Omega polarity in your own being. That is when you have the maximum release of the Godhead. Therefore, part of the Path that we are on is conserving this sacred fire and using it to heal the nations and to rescue souls who might otherwise pass from the screen of life if we were not there to make the call for them.

Dedicate the Solar Plexus as a Place of Peace

So the "place of the sun," the place where Cosmic Christ Peace must be established in you, is in the solar plexus. It is in this very first chakra below the heart where we want to establish a flame of peace and where we determine that we will have absolutely no compromise in our feeling world. We may even take a vow at the altar that we will keep still our solar plexus and not allow ourselves to become emotionally embroiled in the petty situations that come upon us all every day. This is the great work of the Elohim of Peace.

When you accomplish this peace, you will have within you the peace-commanding presence of Almighty God at all times. You just have to dedicate that chakra, that bowl of light, as a place of peace, having the holy waters of peace, the holy fire of peace so that you are ready with that holy fire, you are ready with that holy water of peace at all times.

The Golden Oil of Peace

The Elohim Peace has advised us to "seal your world daily...within a capsule of the golden oil of peace from my very heart, which as a mantle of infinite protection will guard your world."[2] He then asked us to daily bring a portion of this peace into the world of others.

This is an example of an I AM affirmation you can write down based on the words of a dictation:

I AM sealing my world in a capsule of the golden oil of peace from the heart of Elohim Peace as a mantle of infinite protection to guard my world.

If you take that with you and give it every day, you will have the action of Elohim Peace and Aloha in your life.

Peace also instructed us to learn to release the fire of our hearts by giving the mantra

Peace, be still and know that I AM God!

He said, "Learn to release the fire of the heart, the sacred fire, and to be infilled again...with this mantra."[3]

You can say this if you see chaos on television. You can speak it right into the TV. You can speak it into a crowd. You can speak it to a part of your body that is not functioning properly. You can speak it into your household. You can do a clearance of all the rooms of your house and dedicate them to peace and start training your children in accepting that this is a house of peace. We do not argue. We do not accuse. We do not have discord, and so forth. We resolve all matters by the quietness and the all-presence of the power of the flame of peace.

When Peace Has Gone, Everything Has Gone

We have a decree to the "Great Sun Disc" that was taken from a dictation by the Elohim Peace. Peace expressed his desire that all connected with The Summit Lighthouse and with Saint Germain learn how to place the Great Sun Disc over their solar plexus. He said, "I would like you to learn how to magnify the power of that disc of light so that you are not so vulnerable to the onslaughts of others.... When peace has gone, everything has gone and there is nothing left."[4]

Why did he say this? He said it because things fall apart when there is not peace. When there is discord, you cannot hold a matrix, you cannot hold a relationship together, you cannot hold a family together, a nation together.

"When peace has gone, everything has gone.... And only when you come to a point where once again, through the power of interior equilibrium, you have found your balance does the power of peace begin to flow and do you start again to build those wondrous castles in the air—castles of hope—

which may well materialize into the blessings you seek because you have kept the peace."[5]

Decree and Visualization for the Great Sun Disc

Peace said to visualize the Great Sun Disc as a large round shield of heavy armour reflecting in all directions the dazzling light of the Great Central Sun.

GREAT SUN DISC

Beloved mighty I AM Presence, beloved Holy Christ Self and beloved Jesus the Christ: Blaze your dazzling light of a thousand suns in, through and around my four lower bodies as a mighty guardian action of the light of God that never fails to protect the peaceful outpicturing of God's plan through my every thought, word and deed.

Place your Great Sun Disc over my solar plexus as a mighty shield of armour that shall instantaneously deflect all discord whatsoever that may ever be directed against me or the light for which I stand.

I call now in the name of my mighty I AM Presence to the Elohim of Peace to release throughout my entire being and world the necessary action of the mighty flame of Cosmic Christ Peace that shall sustain in me the Christ consciousness at all times, so that I may never be found engaged in a release of misqualified energy to any part of life, whether it be fear, malice, mild dislike, mistrust, censure or disdain.

I call to beloved Saint Germain to seize all energy that I have ever released against my brethren and that has caused them any form of discomfort whatsoever. And in the name of my mighty I AM Presence I command that that energy be removed from their worlds—cause, effect, record and memory—and transmuted by the violet flame into the purity and perfection that is the sacred-fire essence of God, that the earth and all elemental life might be cut free forever from human creation and given their eternal victory in the light!

I accept this done right now with full power! I AM this done right now with full power! I AM, I AM, I AM God-life expressing perfection all ways at all times. This which I call forth for myself I call forth for every man, woman and child on this planet!

Beloved I AM! Beloved I AM! Beloved I AM!

This is what we are intended to be doing with our solar plexus. It is the place of the sun. It's the Son of God, the S-o-n, and it's the S-u-n of the Great Central Sun.

The Great Sun Disc of the solar plexus can beam signals of light across the universe as we use it as a mirror, sending thoughts of victory and hope to those evolutions in other systems of worlds who are battling against spacecraft, extraterrestrials, fallen angels, et cetera. Our work on this planet must give hope to all other planetary systems that there is a way out and that we do not have to be enslaved by fallen angels any longer, no matter from what system we hail. We also have an abbreviated mantra to the Great Sun Disc:

O disc of light from heaven's height,
Descend with all your perfection!
Make my aura bright with freedom's light
And the masters' love and protection!

Give these four lines with the fiery intensity and the visualization that now your solar plexus is a beacon light and it crosses infinity. There is no end to the training and focusing of this beacon.

By feeding the power of the sacred fire from the base chakra, from the I AM Presence, Holy Christ Self and threefold flame, you have the ability to increase your momentum and the action of your decree until evolutions from far-off worlds can receive from your heart love and messages of victory and whatever you would send them that is a positive uplift.

So we own a disc of light, and you can think of it as a sending and receiving station. How can the solar plexus be used for these pure efforts and these pure goals if we're constantly allowing it to get into turmoil and upheaval, et cetera? We can't let this happen.

We either recognize that God placed in our bodies a sending and receiving station—we're sending our prayers to him, receiving the answers back—or we allow it to become a garbage dump for all kinds of emotional nonsense. So that is the choice. If we want our mastery, we know what we will choose.

Jesus' Mantras of Peace

The Elohim Peace has revealed that many of the sayings of Jesus Christ came from him. He said that Jesus learned these sayings "as a disciple of the Elohim Peace long before he took incarnation to be the Prince of Peace."[6]

Peace has told us that Jesus used mantras to "hold the balance for the evolutions of earth." If Jesus used mantras, which are simple one-line prayers, then why should we not do the same and do so continuously? Once you have a momentum on a mantra, whether it is an Eastern mantra or a decree in our decree book,[7] that mantra sings in your heart. And many of you have told me that you awaken in the night hearing yourself reciting your violet-flame mantras and also other mantras.

Peace said that Jesus often used these salutations in honor of the name of Peace: "Peace be unto you." "Fear not, little flock; for it is your Father's good pleasure to give you the kingdom." "Be of good cheer: it is I; be not afraid."[8]

Be the Master of Your World

Peace explained that he has often used our calls "to render a great and untold assistance to the planet," to prevent "many small wars from starting" and to help put out the "fire" of "larger conflagrations." He explained:

> When you master yourself, as the Master Jesus did, you can go to sleep and let others rock the boat for all they are worth, all the while knowing that the sea is God's sea, that the boat is God's boat, that your body is God's temple, that your mind is the dwelling place of God, that your soul is the soul of God, that the wind is his to command, that the wave obeys his voice.
>
> ... Rest in that great cosmic tranquility that refuses to be affrighted, that refuses to be disturbed, regardless of outer conditions. And then you will sleep through the storms of the world or you may remain awake through them; but you will be unaffected by any of them, for you will be the master of your world.[9]

The Warring in our Members

On one occasion, Peace and Aloha told us why war remains on our planet. This is an indictment of all of us. We must listen to it carefully. They said, "The momentums and records of war on planet Earth remain untransmuted because many of the ... ones who have the gift of the violet flame and the Science of the Spoken Word do not use it to transmute, first and foremost, the warring in their own members."[10]

If you have a conflict within your psyche, within yourself, go after it with the violet flame and your calls to Astrea. Do not allow Peace and Aloha to come and find you out of alignment because you have not used the Science of the Spoken Word and the violet flame to take care of these conditions. It takes surrender, profound surrender, to do this. But it is the only way to ride above the wave of the turbulence that can come at the place of the solar plexus.

"In order to make peace with your inner being, you must declare war against the not-self."[11] We have called the not-self the dweller-on-the-threshold, and we have a decree for the binding of our dweller-on-the-threshold. We need to use it daily for ourselves and all members of our household.

I have recommended the dweller-on-the-threshold call to many people. It has saved marriages, saved lives, saved children. It is very important. It's the first place to begin when you're having a problem with any member of your family, your extended family or people with whom you regularly interact, such as those with whom you share office space, with whom you work side by side.

"The defeat of war by all seven Elohim and the entire Spirit of the Great White Brotherhood is tops on our agenda. But ... if the chelas of the light do not take up the dismantling of the components of war in their own psyches and allow them to be consumed, ... where shall we go?"[12]

We Must Be Guardians of Our Energies

Peace and Aloha have explained that "every one of you who has lost that peace for a moment, an hour or a day has contributed in ways small and great to war, to crime, to murder, to mayhem, to cataclysm."[13]

If those to whom the Elohim of Peace are speaking are you who have been Keepers of the Flame who have decreed for many years, then the entire decree momentum that you are using amplifies the warring in your members and will amplify the warring in the earth if you suddenly become discordant. You pay a heavy price and the Elohim, the archangels and the planet pay a very heavy price when spiritual people misuse the light that they have invoked from God.

So understanding the Science of the Spoken Word and practicing it means that we must be guardians of our energies at all times. This is a sacred trust that God has given to us. And we know that the price Saint Germain paid for sponsoring humanity with the violet flame is that he takes upon himself the karma that people make by their misuse of the violet flame. You wouldn't put that burden on your best friend, yet Saint Germain is your best friend because he has given you the gift of freedom and spiritual freedom.

The "acceleration of the Christ consciousness" in all people is "the only solution to war and the only option for peace."[14] You cannot just cast out what is discordant and leave a vacuum. Jesus spoke about a worse thing coming upon a person from whom he had cast out demons:

> When the unclean spirit is gone out of a man, he walketh through dry places, seeking rest; and finding none, he saith, "I will return unto my house whence I came out."
>
> And when he cometh, he findeth it swept and garnished.
>
> Then goeth he, and taketh to him seven other spirits more wicked than himself, and they enter in and dwell there; and the last state of that man is worse than the first.[15]

The point here is that if we leave a vacuum—we clean our house but we don't fill our house with the Christ Presence—then we are vulnerable. So we have to deal with the negatives, but we need to give far more decrees on the positive side and still not neglect challenging the negatives in our world.

Elohim Peace and Aloha have also said that abortion is "the most pressing problem of our time because it is the greatest single act that causes the greatest karma to the individual and to nations."[16]

Become Warriors of Peace

Peace has asked us to become warriors of peace. He said: "War is the agenda of the fallen ones,... war on planet Earth. Disarmament and the seeming disappearance of World Communism does not change that fact in any way. The Buddhas ... [and] the Cosmic Christs are the warriors of peace.... Be champions, warriors of peace and understand that pacifism is a perversion of peace! *Peace* is the guardian action of the sixth ray." Since the sixth ray is the ray of Christhood, then peace is the guardian action of our fulfilling our Christhood on the sixth ray. "*Peace* takes care of life."[17]

So you might read that and give the following mantra:

In the name of my mighty I AM Presence,
in the name Jesus Christ,
I AM a warrior of peace!

To help us accomplish whatever the masters tell us to do, we need to create mantras and give them.

Remember the Sign of Peace—the Abhaya Mudra

Peace and Aloha have explained that they can radiate rings of peace to push back the darkness and the threat of war.

They said, "I must warn you of the forces of anti-peace abroad in the world who will come to challenge my flame in your heart by all manner of subterfuge, serpentine logic and subtlety." Peace and Aloha instructed us, "Remember the sign of peace of the Prince of Peace. Raise the right hand and turn them back! Remember the tube of light and the solar ring and the ring of peace."[18]

The Elohim are referring to the *abhaya* mudra.* The power of peace is an invincible power. You can visualize a ray of white fire coming out of your palm. You can clear an entire audience with one turn of the hand in this manner. You can do this because you have a momentum on drawing forth the sacred fire of your I AM Presence.

I have always used this mudra wherever I've lectured around the world—throughout the United States, in Europe, and so forth. It sets up a protection to the audience as well as a protection to the speaker. You can use it in every type of situation where people are out of control.

Never Take Offense

The Elohim of Peace have warned that our peace is only skin-deep when we become offended at little things and become angry when someone steps on our toes. Many years ago I learned a great lesson on taking offense from the writings of Mary Baker Eddy. And that was the title of the teaching, "Taking Offense." By the time I had read that excerpt from her writings, I realized that there was never any reason in any situation to take offense at what someone might do to me. Since the age of nineteen, I have found it to be a

---

* To form the *abhaya* mudra, raise your right hand to shoulder height with your palm turned outward. Your fingers are extended upward and may be slightly curved.

most liberating state of consciousness to never take offense.

Give only magnanimity, joy, gratitude, love and support to those who may be offending you. It is truly a tremendous liberation. You can learn a lot about yourself and all people if you are never offended, no matter what someone does to you.

Although we may think we have attained to peace, Peace and Aloha have said that "99 percent of your consciousness, your energy, is outside of the flame of peace."[19] This tells us something about the flame of peace and something about ourselves. The flame of peace is tremendously powerful. It is so powerful that we may only have 1 percent of it and still feel a tremendous power of peace in our lives.

We can increase oneness with Peace if we do not take offense. If we don't take offense, we don't have to fight back. We can say something very quieting and calming and simply not be engaged.

Elohim Peace and Aloha said: "You have created your own zoo and you have made yourself the zookeeper instead of the keeper of the flame of peace. And so you guard the animals ... of your human creation [in the subconscious, in the unconscious] that you have fashioned out of your greed and your darkness, your self-concern and your revenge."[20]

You can see all of the weeds we have to pluck out of our gardens, in order to be worthy of walking in the Presence of God as the presence of peace.

Ten Tips for Peace

Over the years the Elohim Peace and Aloha have given many tips to help us keep peace. I'd like to give you ten of these tips.

1. Make the best of things. This takes a very upbeat attitude. When working with others, make the best of each situation. Peace and Aloha have said, "We cannot guarantee perfect people anywhere.... Do not lament another's shortcomings, but by the flame of peace supply the difference!"[21]

Supply the difference that someone you are working with may not have a talent for, an energy for, a desire for. Make up the difference. Make the best of things.

"Give of your heart and see how the blossoms of peace spring forth in the hearts of [others].... Serve the Christ in them and see how they will respond."[22]

2. Write down the situations of nonresolution in your day planners. This can be knotty, because every time you open your day planner, you're going to see the lists of nonresolution and you're going to want to get rid of those things. And therefore, you have to come to resolution with whomever you do not already have resolution.

Use your day planner "to write down those situations of nonresolution in your life.... Wherever there is a heart that daily does note in his [preferred] planner such nonresolutions and does determine to achieve resolution within himself and with others by sunset, there is a heart that rests in the heart of the Prince of Peace."[23] And that is a wonderful blessing.

So I wrote a mantra for myself that you can also use:

> *In the name of my mighty I AM Presence,*
> *I rest in the heart of the Prince of Peace.*

"Rejoice to check off each day that you have said,

> *Peace, be still! Peace, be still! Peace, be still*
> *and know that I AM God!*

or when you can say at the end of that day, 'Truly I have not allowed an incorrect vibration to emanate from this place of the sun (the solar-plexus chakra).'"[24]

Who are you talking to when you say "Peace, be still and

know that I AM God!"? You are talking to your feeling
world. You are talking to something that's in your carnal
mind. You are talking to something in yourself that is not
whole, that is not at peace. And you are commanding your
atoms, cells and electrons, the organs of your body and your
four lower bodies to be still and stop complaining and stop
constantly nagging and saying, "Give me this. Give me that.
I want this. I want that." You are in the peace-commanding
presence of your Holy Christ Self and you are the authority
over all elements of your lower self through Christ.

3. Forgive and ask to be forgiven. Peace and Aloha say,
"Forgive and ask to be forgiven even when you think you are
not in the wrong. Do this because you live by the master's
code of forgiveness. Do it to give another the opportunity to
do the same."[25]

Perhaps you know that someone else may need to be
forgiven or to forgive. By bringing up the subject and being
the first to express it, you make it very easy for another to
apologize or to be forgiven.

4. Remember your vow. "Remember your determination
and even your vow, if you have made it, that you will not be
moved from the God-centeredness of love and peace, come
what may, even in trifling matters. For have not trifling
matters ignited world wars?"[26]

5. Seek daily resolution by giving the violet flame. Peace
and Aloha said: "Seek daily resolution. Put everything into the
violet flame!... Examine the rightness of your heart daily to
be certain that you have not left frayed edges in any
relationship, that you have not abruptly parted from someone
without resolution, that you have not left any matter hanging,
such as a simple disagreement or discourtesy."[27]

Examine your heart. Sometimes people have the idea that
the heart is perfect. The heart needs perfecting just as every

other chakra needs perfecting. When we want to give love to someone, we call to our Holy Christ Self to send the love of the Sacred Heart of our Holy Christ Self to that person.

We must not assume that our hearts are pure. I think it is a misconception when people in the New Age movement say, "I'm speaking from my heart" and automatically assume "My heart is pure and therefore you can trust what I'm saying."

We have to purify all of our being, including our heart. The heart is very burdened with its envy, with its jealousy, with its anger. All kinds of vibrations are in people's hearts, as well as sluggishness from a lifetime of wrong eating. And the fat that covers over the heart is also a block to the flow.

So when we send blessings to people, let us remember to send blessings from our Holy Christ Self and our I AM Presence. And let us continue our daily use of Saint Germain's Heart Meditations[28] that we might perfect our hearts.

6. Be humble. This is a wonderful state of being, the state of being humble and of having humility. "Be humble before your God. Don't be a know-it-all but ... have a sense of holiness in the presence of one another's Christ Self and a sense of the holiness of the flame that burns in the heart of the one that sits next to you."[29]

When we say, "Be humble," the corollary is "Judge not." When we judge others, we are engaging in pride.

7. Forsake harshness. Peace said, "Forsake the jagged ways, the abrupt motions, the absence of grace and the harshness and the cruelty of the word idly spoken, for all of these are an offense to Elohim."[30]

8. Do not chatter or criticize. "Take some moments each day to celebrate the vibration of soundlessness." "Take a vow of silence from senseless chattering."[31] Do not engage in criticism and backbiting.

9. Make your body a chalice for light—every cell, every organ, the etheric, mental, desire and physical bodies. Peace said that we should make every molecule of our body a chalice for light.

"Solve the chemistry of being here below and the biochemistry.... You are made of points of light.... Seek the divine harmony ... of all atoms and cells ... and all organs in your being with one another and with the etheric matrix.... Find that equilibrium.... Become alchemists of your own temple. See how much more of God you can hold within the chakras, organs and all the components of being."[32]

10. Keep the peace with one another. Peace said, "Receive the gentle rebuke from anyone of this community when you abandon your point of peace."[33]

Do Not React when Someone Reminds You to Return to Your Center

Here I should remind you not to take offense. If someone comes along and lets you know that you have a fault that they would like to tell you about, they may be right or they may be wrong; but you should always consider what they have to say.

I have learned the best lessons about myself from my enemies. I always listen to what my enemies say to me and about me. And I weigh whether or not what they have said is something that I should examine in myself and correct. We all need to do this.

I know that in the community here and throughout the world, there are many people who don't take kindly to another Keeper of the Flame mentioning to them that they might benefit from changing their ways in this or that matter.

Elohim Peace said, "Remind one another, regardless of rank or position or background or standing, that where there is the breaking of harmony and the breaking of peace there is the fracturing of the mandala" of the entire community throughout the world. "Do not react when someone … reminds you to return to your center," to your centeredness in God. "Take the reminder and thank that one with all your heart. Call immediately upon the law of forgiveness.... The byword of the peacemakers is 'I shall not be moved.' "[34] And putting that in a mantra, we would say,

> *In the name of my mighty I AM Presence,*
> *I shall not be moved!*

How to Counsel Someone

When you want to counsel someone, first take a step backward and say:

> **Peace, be still and know that the I AM God in me is the I AM God in that one. And I go forth to establish Christ Peace, to teach a lesson, to correct an error. Therefore, O God, seal me in my tube of light, the violet flame, the mantle and the armour of God that I speak the word of truth and yet hold the God-harmony of peace.**

"Think what a magnet this shall be," said Elohim Peace. "It shall be the greatest anti-war manifestation on the face of planet Earth! This is my prediction and my prophecy! Will you make it come true?"[35]

I would like to point out to you that when we are in the retreats of the ascended masters in the etheric octave, none of us is better than another. We are souls naked. We go to the retreats in our etheric body. We sit in halls of learning. We study under the great adepts, the Elohim and the archangels.

When we return to our work in this octave, some have high positions, some have what would be considered lowly positions, some take on greater burdens than others. But we have to remember that no matter how important we are in our daily service and work, when it comes to our spiritual path, we are all simply souls striving for the same goal. And we all have gifts to give to one another. So when we speak to someone who is above us in the hierarchy of an organization, it is not in the sense that we are challenging them but in the sense that we are speaking to their soul.

It is always polite to say to someone, "May I tell you something that I think would be helpful to you?" And open the way in great kindness and softness if you wish to express something that you feel will help that person. If you are in error and another person is on the receiving end of your error, that person should be just as gracious and thank you for your concern and for your words.

In Time of Distress, Visualize the Pavilion of Peace

Elohim Peace has delivered a dictation in which he gave a dispensation and a mantra. He placed a miniature replica of the Temple of Peace in the hearts of those present, and he said, "All you have to do when all around you is turbulent and you are in distress and in confusion is to visualize in miniature the Pavilion of Peace. Call unto me and unto your individualized God Presence, and say:

I need thee every hour, O Elohim of Peace and beloved mighty I AM Presence! Show forth thy light!

"And with the words 'Show forth thy light,' I will come again and create the vibratory action of my peace."[36]

What We Do on Earth Affects the Heaven-World

Peace and Aloha have promised us that heaven will

reward our efforts to sustain peace and pass our tests. They said: "Make your peace with all people. For you cannot make lasting progress on the Path until you do.... Know that God does test every living soul. Be willing, then, to pass those tests and to exercise ingenuity of heart in so doing.... For every individual upon earth who is right with God,... there shall be added ten thousand angels unto the bands of the legions of the sixth ray of the Lord Jesus Christ ministering to the peoples of planet Earth."[37]

This teaches us the profound lesson that what we do on earth affects the heaven-world. And for each one of us who is mirroring the blessings of heaven here below and embodying those blessings, God will send ten thousand angels.

Win Your Victory Every Day

It is the Divine Mother who leads us into battle against the forces of evil. You can placate an enemy. You can placate one of your own bad habits and just not really fight it and exorcise it and get rid of it. People can live a whole lifetime crying "Peace, peace," and they have no peace because they are afraid to go to war and exorcise and defeat the enemy within and without. I say to you that anyone who does not exorcise that enemy of discord, defiance, internal division within himself is a coward. And cowards are the ones who sustain an unlawful peace, which is no peace.

Jesus said, "I came not to send peace, but a sword."[38] The only peace we can ever have is the peace of resolution, the peace of honor that comes in the white fire of the base chakra. It's not the peace of the world that compromises to obtain a certain resolution, a certain standoff, but it is the peace of wholeness that demands, absolutely demands, that we cast into the sacred fire all anti-peace, all inharmony, the synthetic self, the dweller.

Go out and settle for nothing less than peace that you win in your life because you chain that dweller-on-the-threshold, you put him behind bars, triple bars, and he's not allowed to act in your world. Then you will know such peace because every single day of your life you will mount the ladder of the Tree of Life.

Decrees and Mantras

VIOLET FIRE AND TUBE OF LIGHT DECREE
by Saint Germain

O my constant, loving I AM Presence, thou light of God above me whose radiance forms a circle of fire before me to light my way:

I AM faithfully calling to thee to place a great pillar of light from my own mighty I AM God Presence all around me right now today! Keep it intact through every passing moment, manifesting as a shimmering shower of God's beautiful light through which nothing human can ever pass. Into this beautiful electric circle of divinely charged energy direct a swift upsurge of the violet fire of freedom's forgiving transmuting flame!

Cause the ever expanding energy of this flame projected downward into the forcefield of my human energies to completely change every negative condition into the positive polarity of my own great God Self! Let the magic of its mercy so purify my world with light that all whom I contact shall always be blessed with the fragrance of violets from God's own heart in memory of the blessed dawning day when all discord—cause, effect, record and memory—is forever changed into the victory of light and the peace of the ascended Jesus Christ.

I AM now constantly accepting the full power and manifestation of this fiat of light and calling it into instantaneous action by my own God-given free will and the power to accelerate without limit this sacred release of assistance from God's own heart until all men are ascended and God-free in the light that never, never, never fails!

DECREES FOR PROTECTION

In the name of Almighty God, in the name of Almighty God, in the name of Almighty God, I call for the full power of the light of God that never, never, never fails to give earth her victory now!

———————

Lord Michael before, Lord Michael behind,
Lord Michael to the right, Lord Michael to the left,
Lord Michael above, Lord Michael below,
Lord Michael, Lord Michael wherever I go!
I AM his love protecting here!
I AM his love protecting here!
I AM his love protecting here!

———————

I AM Presence, thou art Master,
I AM Presence, clear the way!
Let thy light and all thy power
Take possession here this hour!
Charge with victory's mastery,
Blaze blue lightning, blaze thy substance!
Into this thy form descend,
That perfection and its glory
Shall blaze forth and earth transcend!

I AM THE VIOLET FLAME

In the name of the beloved mighty victorious Presence of God, I AM in me, and my very own beloved Holy Christ Self, I call to beloved Alpha and Omega in the heart of God in our Great Central Sun, beloved Saint Germain, beloved Portia, beloved Lanello, the entire Spirit of the Great White Brotherhood and the World Mother, elemental life—fire, air, water and earth!

To expand the violet flame within my heart, purify my four lower bodies, transmute all misqualified energy I have ever imposed upon life, and blaze mercy's healing ray throughout the earth, the elementals, and all mankind and answer this my call infinitely, presently, and forever:

> I AM the violet flame
> In action in me now
> I AM the violet flame
> To light alone I bow
> I AM the violet flame
> In mighty cosmic power
> I AM the light of God
> Shining every hour
> I AM the violet flame
> Blazing like a sun
> I AM God's sacred power
> Freeing every one

And in full faith I consciously accept this manifest, manifest, manifest! (3x) right here and now with full power, eternally sustained, all-powerfully active, ever expanding and world enfolding until all are wholly ascended in the light and free!

Beloved I AM! Beloved I AM! Beloved I AM!

THE LAW OF FORGIVENESS

Beloved mighty victorious Presence of God, I AM in me, beloved Holy Christ Self, beloved Heavenly Father, beloved great Karmic Board, beloved Kuan Yin, Goddess of Mercy, beloved Lanello, the entire Spirit of the Great White Brotherhood and the World Mother, elemental life—fire, air, water, and earth!

In the name and by the power of the Presence of God which I AM and by the magnetic power of the sacred fire vested in me, I call upon the law of forgiveness and the violet transmuting flame for each transgression of thy Law, each departure from thy sacred covenants. Restore in me the Christ mind, forgive my wrongs and unjust ways, make me obedient to thy code, let me walk humbly with thee all my days.

In the name of the Father, the Mother, the Son and the Holy Spirit, I decree for all whom I have ever wronged and for all who have ever wronged me:

> Violet fire,* enfold us! (3x)
> Violet fire, hold us! (3x)
> Violet fire, set us free! (3x)
> I AM, I AM, I AM surrounded by
> a pillar of violet flame,*
> I AM, I AM, I AM abounding in
> pure love for God's great name,
> I AM, I AM, I AM complete
> by thy pattern of perfection so fair,
> I AM, I AM, I AM God's radiant flame
> of love gently falling through the air.
> Fall on us! (3x)
> Blaze through us! (3x)
> Saturate us! (3x)

And in full faith...

* "Mercy's flame" or "purple flame" may be used for "violet flame."

POUR OUT THE RADIANT GOLDEN OIL OF PEACE!
by the Elohim of Peace

Beloved mighty Presence of God, I AM in me, and beloved Elohim of Peace: from the zenith of the heavens pour out the radiant golden oil of peace unto the horizon of my world to the 360 degrees of the circumference of my being that extends to the borders of time and eternity!

Fill the circle of my world and the worlds of all children of the light with such an effulgent light and love as is the manifest power of the Elohim of Peace that no dissonance or any other variant of peace can manifest where I AM in the heart of Peace!

MANTRA: *Beloved Elohim of Peace:*
From the zenith of the heavens,
Pour out the radiant golden oil of peace
Unto the horizon of my world! (9x)

The Elohim of Peace, August 7, 1958, Philadelphia

THE PATH OF THE ELOHIM OF PEACE
by the Elohim of Peace

Enough! I have had done with my human creation and I choose to enter the path of the Elohim of Peace! I choose to now receive the original endowment of peace that Elohim Peace gave upon the founding of this organization.

I shall become that point of peace to which every angel ministering on earth shall have recourse. Yes, in my heart the flame of peace shall abide. Therefore I shall be unmoved. I shall not be moved by what does transpire anywhere outside the circle of my being or within it.

This day I have said: Enough is enough! I am the victim of my own wrong desiring. I am the victim of my abuse of my four lower bodies. I am the victim of my karma. And this day I say, I shall no longer be the victim of myself but I shall be the instrument of God!

I shall walk out from this court of King Arthur and I shall keep my vow to keep my counsel, keep my peace, keep the sealing of my words and to control the flashing forth of dark thought or feeling and the revolving of negative spirals of the memory.

I can do all of this, for I am the child of the heart of El Morya, my beloved. I can do all of this because my God is with me. I have a path, I have Maitreya, I have a messenger whom I can see and touch and who will love me and comfort me and help me and rebuke me and lead me.

Yes, I am in the best possible position that my karma allows me to be in. For I know there is no injustice anywhere in the universe and I am truly convinced that there is mercy beyond mercy that I have this opportunity this day to remake myself by the power of Elohim in the image and likeness of Almighty God, by the power of the Word with Brahman in the Beginning.

Yes, I will work with Elohim of Peace. And I know that because God sent Elohim to endow this activity that this activity is sponsored from the Elohimic level and all the power of Elohim is upon me and the mighty chalice of the resurrection flame in the Heart of the Inner Retreat.

Yes, I shall take the dispensations of Elohim, for they are power in the seven rays. They are the power of Alpha and Omega. And I shall remake myself that I might carry the spiral of the next thirty three years of this activity until The Summit Lighthouse transcends the octaves here below as Above and its beams shed their powerful light into the depths of Death and

Hell so that souls caught in those levels may follow the beam to the heart of their I AM Presence and receive the archangels' deliverance.

Yes, I will walk in the living flame of peace. I shall be a **true pilgrim of peace. And I shall show the two-edged sword dividing the Real from the unreal, binding the engines and elements of war.**

Yes, I know the meaning of true peace and I know it is not pacifism. I know that the power of peace will swallow up the records of war upon this planet as I take the mantra: **Peace, be still and know that I AM God! (4x)**

MANTRA:

> *Enough! I have had done with my human creation*
> *And I choose to enter the path of the Elohim of Peace!*
> *Yes, I will walk in the living flame of peace.*
> *I shall be a true pilgrim of peace.*
> *And I shall show the two-edged sword*
> *Dividing the Real from the unreal,*
> *Binding the engines and elements of war.*
> *Peace, be still and know that I AM God!* (4x)   (9x)

The Elohim of Peace, August 11, 1991, Royal Teton Ranch

Note: After you have given these decrees for a while in their entirety, you may wish to give the abbreviated mantra that is printed in italic at the end of each decree.

AFFIRMATIONS OF PEACE

I AM sealing my world
in a capsule of the golden oil of peace
from the heart of Elohim Peace
as a mantle of infinite protection to guard my world.

Peace, be still!
Peace, be still!
Peace, be still
and know that I AM God!

In the name of my mighty I AM Presence,
In the name Jesus Christ,
I AM a warrior of peace!

In the name of my mighty I AM Presence,
I rest in the heart of the Prince of Peace.

In the name of my mighty I AM Presence,
I shall not be moved!

I need thee every hour, O Elohim of Peace and beloved
mighty I AM Presence! Show forth thy Light!

O disc of light from heaven's height,
Descend with all your perfection!
Make my aura bright with freedom's light
And the masters' love and protection!

I AM God's awareness of
peace and love, ministration and service.

Peace, be still and know that the I AM God in me is the I AM God in that one. And I go forth to establish Christ Peace, to teach a lesson, to correct an error. Therefore, O God, seal me in my tube of light, the violet flame, the mantle and the armour of God that I speak the word of truth and yet hold the God-harmony of peace.

These additional decrees and mantras can be found on the following pages of this book:

NOTES

Books referenced in these notes are published by Summit University Press unless otherwise indicated.

INTRODUCTION

1. Rom. 7:19, 21.
2. Rom. 8:7.

CHAPTER ONE: REMEMBER THE ANCIENT ENCOUNTER

This dictation by Kuthumi was delivered on January 27, 1985, at Camelot, Los Angeles County, California. It has been previously published in *Pearls of Wisdom,* vol. 28, no. 9, March 3, 1985.

1. Kuthumi, who once walked the path of Christian sainthood as Francis of Assisi (c. 1181–1226), was revered in his soul's final incarnation, in the nineteenth century, as the Kashmiri Brahman Koot Hoomi Lal Singh—known to students of Theosophy as the Master K.H. Together with El Morya (the Master M.), he founded the Theosophical Society through H. P. Blavatsky in 1875. The Masters M. and K.H. wrote *The Mahatma Letters* between 1880 and 1884 to A. P. Sinnett, a disciple in the Theosophical Society. In the service preceding Kuthumi's dictation, the messenger read from Section III, "Probation and Chelaship" (Letters XL, XLIX, LV), in which Morya and Koot Hoomi speak of the malice and intrigue surrounding the Theosophical Society from various sources, including the press and Christians.
2. Heb. 7:1–3.
3. Ps. 110:4; Heb. 5:5–10; 6:19, 20; Heb. 7:14–22.
4. Matt. 18:14; John 17:12; 2 Thess. 2:3, 4.
5. Matt. 24:22; Mark 13:20.
6. The electronic belt is the negative spiral or forcefield of density that surrounds the lower portion of man's physical form and is created through his misqualification of energy. Extending from

the waist to beneath the feet, the electronic belt is similar in shape to a large kettledrum and contains the aggregate records of an individual's negative thoughts and feelings. It is the perversion of the causal body, electronic rings of rainbow light surrounding the I AM Presence (the upper figure in the Chart of Your Divine Self). This is man's "cosmic bank account" where energy he has positively qualified is stored and becomes a part of his immortal identity. Thus Jesus admonished his disciples to "lay up for yourselves treasures in heaven..." (Matt. 6:20). See Mark and Elizabeth Prophet, *The Path of the Higher Self* (2003), pp. 268–77.

7. 1 Cor. 3:13–15; 1 Pet. 1:7; 4:12.

8. Isa. 34:8; 61:2; 63:4; Jer. 50:15, 28; 51:6, 11; Luke 21:22.

9. John 8:23.

10. Matt. 25:1–13.

11. Matt. 14:28–31

12. Gen. 4:3–8

13. Jesus and Kuthumi, *Prayer and Meditation* (1995).

14. The term *indulgence* in Roman Catholicism refers to the plenary (full) or partial remission of temporal punishment due for sins whose guilt and eternal punishment have already been pardoned. Indulgences are usually granted in exchange for prayers and devotional acts. During the medieval period, this practice came under abuse when indulgences could be obtained through monetary contributions. This was one of the grievances that eventually instigated the Protestant Reformation.

CHAPTER TWO: YOUR DIVINE INHERITANCE

1. Ps. 91:1, 2.

2. Exod. 3:13–15.

3. Gen. 4:26; 12:8; 26:25; Ps. 99:6; Joel 2:32; Acts 2:21; Rom. 10:12, 13.

4. Exod. 13:21, 22; Num. 14:14; Neh. 9:12, 19; Ps. 78:14.

5. Matt. 6:19, 20; John 14:2.

6. Matt. 6:21; Luke 12:34.

7. Rev. 10:1.

8. John 1:3–9.

9. The Nicene Creed.

10. Col. 2:9.

11. Jer. 23:5, 6; 33:15, 16.

12. Rom. 8:14 17; Gal. 3:26 29; 4:4 7.
13. James 4:8.
14. Eccles. 12:6.
15. Rev. 22:1.
16. Matt. 3:16, 17; 17:5; Mark 1:10, 11; Luke 3:21, 22; 2 Pet. 1:17, 18; Matt. 12:18; Isa. 42:1.
17. Prov. 26:11.
18. Matt. 18:22.
19. See the Lord's Prayer. Matt. 6:9–15; Mark 11:25, 26; Luke 11:1–4.
20. John 1:11–13.
21. Phil. 2:12.
22. John 1:5.
23. Matt. 7:15.
24. Zech. 13:7; Matt. 26:31; Mark 14:27.
25. Ps. 82:6 (see Jerusalem Bible); John 10:34.

CHAPTER THREE: THE CREATURE THAT WAS, THAT IS,
AND THAT IS TO COME

This chapter is excerpted from a lecture by Mark L. Prophet delivered on February 20, 1966, in Colorado Springs, Colorado.

1. 1 Cor. 13:4, 5.
2. Prov. 23:7.
3. Ps. 121:4.
4. Gargantua the Great was one of the featured attractions in Ringling Bros. and Barnum & Bailey Circus in the 1930s and 1940s. Gargantua was a 500-pound lowland gorilla, billed as "The Largest Gorilla Ever Exhibited" and "The World's Most Terrifying Living Creature."
5. John 14:30.
6. 1 Pet. 4:5.
7. 1 John 3:2.

CHAPTER FOUR: ARCHETYPES OF THE DWELLER

This chapter is excerpted from a lecture by Elizabeth Clare Prophet delivered on November 26, 1987, in Washington, D.C.

1. Edward Bulwer Lytton, *Zanoni* (Blauvet, N.Y.: Rudolf Steiner Publications, 1971).

2. The Great Divine Director gives further explanation of this point in his series on *The Mechanization Concept,* published in *Pearls of Wisdom,* 1965.
3. Robert Louis Stevenson, *Dr. Jekyll and Mr. Hyde* (New York: Bantam Books, 1981), pp. 83, 86–87, 88–90, 92, 99–100.
4. Rev. 21:7.
5. Rev. 21:8.
6. 1 John 2:15–18.

CHAPTER FIVE: THE LOST TEACHINGS OF JESUS
ON THE ENEMY WITHIN

This chapter is excerpted from a lecture by Elizabeth Clare Prophet delivered on November 26, 1987, in Washington, D.C.

1. Rom. 7:14–25.
2. Eph. 4:22–24; Rom. 8:6.
3. Jesus Christ, October 4, 1987, "The Call of the Cosmic Christ," in *Pearls of Wisdom,* vol. 30, no. 56, November 25, 1987.
4. Jesus Christ, November 1, 1987, "The Day of Thy Christhood," in *Pearls of Wisdom,* vol. 30, no. 74, December 13, 1987.
5. Hans Jonas, *The Gnostic Religion* (Boston: Beacon Press, 1963), p. 34.
6. Tertullian, *On Prescription Against Heretics,* 7.
7. Phil. 2:12
8. Coptic Gnostic Library Project, *The Nag Hammadi Library in English* (San Francisco: Harper & Row, 1978), pp. 140, 137.
9. Exod. 33:20.
10. *The Nag Hammadi Library in English,* p. 117
11. Ibid., p. 118.
12. Ibid., p. 356.
13. Elaine Pagels, *The Gnostic Gospels* (New York: Random House, 1979), p. 152.
14. *The Nag Hammadi Library in English,* p. 125.
15. Matt. 6:24.
16. *The Nag Hammadi Library in English,* p. 149.
17. Robert McQueen Grant, *Gnosticism and Early Christianity* (New York: Harper, 1966), p. 80.
18. G.R.S. Mead, trans., *Pistis Sophia: A Gnostic Gospel* (Blauvelt, N.Y: Spiritual Science Library, 1984), pp. 278, 279.
19. Ibid., pp. 279, 280, 281.

20. Ibid., pp. 235, 236, 238.
21. Ibid., pp. 238, 239.
22. Ibid., p. 239.
23. Ibid., pp. 247, 248–49.
24. Ibid., p. 249.
25. Luke 12:49.
26. Job 19:26.
27. Mead, *Pistis Sophia*, pp. 249–50.
28. Matt. 10:34.
29. Jean Doresse, *The Secret Books of the Egyptian Gnostics* (Rochester, Vt.: Inner Traditions, 1986), p. 23.
30. Mead, *Fragments of a Faith Forgotten*, pp. 276–77.
31. G. de Purucker, *Occult Glossary: A Compendium of Oriental and Theosophical Terms* (Pasadena, Calif.: Theosophical University Press, 1969), pp. 40–41.

CHAPTER SIX: THE AWAKENING OF THE
DWELLER-ON-THE-THRESHOLD

This dictation by Jesus Christ was delivered on March 13, 1983, at Camelot, Los Angeles County, California. It has been previously published in *Pearls of Wisdom,* vol. 26, no. 36, September 4, 1983.

1. Dan. 12:2
2. See ch. 1, note 6.
3. Col. 3:3.
4. Rev. 15:2; 12:10, 11.
5. Matt. 25:1-13.
6. Matt. 4:1–11; Luke 4:1–13.
7. See Jesus Christ, February 1, 1982, "The Final Judgment of Satan," in *Pearls of Wisdom,* vol. 25, no. 16, February 1, 1982.
8. Rev. 14:1-5.
9. 2 Cor. 6:14.
10. On October 10, 1971, the Great Divine Director said: "Look at yourselves now—how you have reaped the cycles of karma that you have sown. Must you stand there and allow them to continue on their course? Indeed not, for you are a co-creator!

   "Ask then the Almighty to arrest those cycles not of the light that are continuing in the world, in your consciousness, and in the planetary body. For the mighty I AM Presence has the authority and the power to instantaneously arrest and reverse any cycle and to cause a complete erasing, a disintegration of it, right back to the twelve o'clock line.

"It is as though you would see a moving picture in reverse. All of a sudden, the figures go back into their little holes from which they came, and they reverse the order of their activities. This is the process of transmutation. This is how energy is freed of an imperfect cycle.

"I say to you, you must demand and command it in the name of the Christ—that every single cycle of every single cell and atom within your form that is not outpicturing the perfect cycles of the Christ consciousness is now dissolved, is now arrested and turned back by the authority of your God Presence!

"If you will but make that invocation each morning, you will find in a very short time that only the cycles of immortal life and your divine plan fulfilled and your ascension will prevail. And then the needless draining of energy into the subconscious reaches of your mind—whereby most people drain seventy-five percent or more of their daily allotment into needless, useless patterns and cycles long outworn—will be liberated for the perfectionment of the earth and of your life.

"This is why an avatar, a Christ, is born when a threefold flame is balanced. This is why one man focusing the power of God is all that is required by the hierarchy for the salvation of a planet. For such tremendous energies are liberated by the consciousness that is one-pointed that I cannot tell you how important it is to undo every thread that you have sewn in ignorance and in error...."

11. Luke 21:26.
12. Sanat Kumara (from the Sanskrit, meaning 'always a youth') is the Ancient of Days, spoken of in Daniel 7:9, 13, 22.
13. Luke 21:22.
14. Matt. 24:34; Luke 21:32.
15. Rom. 8:1–13.

CHAPTER SEVEN: CHRIST AND THE DWELLER

This lecture was delivered by Elizabeth Clare Prophet on April 4, 1983, at Camelot, Los Angeles County, California. It has been previously published in *Pearls of Wisdom*, vol. 26, no. 38, September 18, 1983.

1. Acts 7:58–60; 8:1–3; 9:1–31; 13–28.
2. Rom. 8:6, 7.
3. Josh. 24:15.
4. Matt. 4:1–11.
5. In *Fallen Angels and the Origins of Evil,* Elizabeth Clare Prophet discusses the fall of two separate groups of angels—the Nephilim and the Watchers. The Nephilim ("those who were made to fall") are those who were "cast out" of heaven because of their prideful rebellion (Rev. 12:7–9). The Watchers, as revealed in the Book of Enoch, descended of their own accord through inordinate lust for the daughters of men.
6. John 14:30.
7. 1 Tim. 5:24.
8. John 10:30.
9. Luke 22:53.
10. Rom. 8:7; Rev. 2:9; 3:9.
11. Matt. 8:12; 22:13; 25:30; Rev. 2:11; 20:6, 14; 21:8.
12. 1 Cor. 2:14–16.
13. Matt. 23:15; Luke 11:52.
14. Col. 1:27.
15. Mark 4:25.
16. Ps. 94:3.
17. John 9:39.
18. Matt. 6:23.
19. Luke 16:8; Matt. 10:16.
20. Kundalini: lit., "coiled-up serpent"; coiled energy in latency at the base-of-the-spine chakra; the seal of the seed atom; negative polarity in Matter of the positive Spirit-fire that descends from the I AM Presence to the heart chakra. When the Kundalini is awakened (through specific yogic techniques, spiritual disciplines, or intense love of God) it begins to ascend the spinal column through the channels of the *Ida, Pingala,* and *Sushumna,* penetrating and activating each of the chakras. The initiate who has taken the left-handed path at the Y uses the Kundalini to enhance his adeptship in the black arts. The false guru initiates the unwary in the rites of raising the Kundalini before the rituals of soul purification and transmutation of the chakras have taken place. This can result in insanity, demon possession or uncontrolled and inordinate sexual desire or a perversion of the life-force in all the chakras. The One Sent takes his disciples by the hand and leads them gently in the

disciplines of self-mastery until they can deal with the great powers conferred by the Goddess Kundalini and use them to bless and heal all life by the release of the sacred fire through all of the chakras—centering in the heart, which in the true initiate becomes the chalice for the Sacred Heart of Jesus Christ. The Kundalini is the life-force, the Mother energy. When the base chakra and the Kundalini are mastered, they become the vessels for the ascension flame in the one preparing for this initiation.

21. Matt. 13:24–30, 36–43.
22. John 5:22.
23. 1 Cor. 6:2, 3.
24. Matt. 19:28.
25. Luke 22:28–30.
26. John 20:22, 23.
27. Rom. 12:21.
28. James 4:3.
29. 1 John 3:22; 5:14.
30. Matt. 24:22.
31. 1 Pet. 1:5.
32. Thomas Jefferson, letter to Benjamin Rush, September 23, 1800. This statement is carved at the base of the dome, interior of the Jefferson Memorial, Washington, D.C.
33. Dan. 12:1–3.
34. John 10:10.
35. Deut. 4:24.

CHAPTER EIGHT: THE PERSONAL AND PLANETARY
CONSCIOUSNESS OF THE DWELLER-ON-THE-THRESHOLD

This chapter is excerpted from a lecture by Elizabeth Clare Prophet was delivered on April 17, 1983, at Camelot, Los Angeles County, California.

1. Biographical information about Lord Himalaya and the other ascended masters mentioned in this book may be found in Mark L. Prophet and Elizabeth Clare Prophet, *The Masters and Their Retreats* (2003).
2. John 5:22.
3. Acts 1:10.
4. Luke 1:11–20, 26–38.
5. Matt. 23:39; Luke 13:35.

6. In *The Twelfth Planet*, Zecharia Sitchin describes ancient Sumerian tablets that depict an extraterrestrial, super-race of gods called Nephilim (Hebrew, "those who fell," or "those who were cast down") who came to earth in spacecraft 450,000 years ago. After studying the earth to find an area suitable for spacecraft landings and colonization, the Nephilim, according to Sitchin, settled in Mesopotamia. Sitchin describes a "central group" of principal deities: "The head of this family of Gods of Heaven and Earth was AN (or Anu in the Babylonian/Assyrian texts). He was the Great Father of the Gods, the King of the Gods.... The second most powerful deity of the Sumerian pantheon was EN.LIL. His name meant 'lord of the air-space'.... He was Anu's eldest son, born at his father's Heavenly Abode.... The third Great God of Sumer was another son of Anu; he bore two names, E.A ['house water'] and EN.KI ['lord of Earth']. Like his brother Enlil, he, too, was a God of Heaven and Earth." (*The Twelfth Planet* [New York: Avon Books, 1976], pp. 89–102.
7. Luke 19:13.
8. Rev. 4.
9. For more information about the twelve solar hierarchies, the positive and negative qualities of each line, and the use of the science of the cosmic clock, see Elizabeth Clare Prophet, *Predict Your Future: Understand the Cycles of the Cosmic Clock* (2004).
10. The planetary energies of karma and mankind's misqualification of the light return according to cycles. The time of transition from the age of Pisces to the age of Aquarius is a period when mankind's karma, held in abeyance for centuries under the great mercy of the Law, is released for balance according to the cycles of the initiations of the solar hierarchies (charted on the cosmic clock). This period of accelerated karmic return, known as the Dark Cycle, began on April 23, 1969, with the line of Capricorn and advanced one line of the clock each year. April 17, 1983 (the date of this lecture) was therefore at the conclusion of the line of Aquarius; the Dark Cycle in Pisces commenced on April 23, 1983. Aquarius is the line of God-love, and misqualifica-tions of the energies of that line of the clock are described as hatred, mild dislike and witchcraft. Pisces is the line of God-mastery; misqualification of the light of Pisces manifest as fear, doubt, human questioning and records of death. For additional

information about the cosmic clock, see Elizabeth Clare Prophet, *Predict Your Future.*
11. John 9:39.
12. Matt. 21:12–13; Mark 11:15–17.
13. See chapter 6, note 5; Gen. 6:2.
14. See Kuthumi and Djwal Kul, *The Human Aura* (1996), book 2, chapter 8.

CHAPTER NINE: FILLING THE VACUUM

1. Matt. 13:24–30.
2. Rom. 7:23.

CHAPTER TEN: TEN KEYS FOR FINDING PEACE WITHIN

This chapter is excerpted from a lecture by Elizabeth Clare Prophet delivered April 13, 1995, at the Royal Teton Ranch, Park County, Montana. It has been previously published in *Pearls of Wisdom,* vol. 44, nos. 48 and 49, December 2 and 9, 2001. The concluding paragraphs are compiled from lectures delivered June 7, 1983, and July 20, 1993.

1. Peace and Aloha, October 11, 1996, "We Bid You Keep the Flame of Peace," in *Pearls of Wisdom,* vol. 45, no. 41, October 13, 2002.
2. Peace, February 15, 1959.
3. Peace, August 11, 1991, "I Inaugurate a Thirty-Three-Tiered Spiral of Peace in The Summit Lighthouse," in *Pearls of Wisdom,* vol. 34, no. 48, October 13, 1991.
4. Elohim Peace, January 3, 1965.
5. Ibid.
6. Peace and Aloha, June 12, 1976, "I Came Not to Send Peace, but a Sword," in *Pearls of Wisdom,* vol. 21, no. 16, April 16, 1978.
7. See *Prayers, Meditations, Dynamic Decrees for the Coming Revolution in Higher Consciousness* (Corwin Springs, Mont.: The Summit Lighthouse).
8. Peace, January 3, 1965.
9. Ibid.
10. Peace and Aloha, April 8, 1993, "The Path of True Love," in *Pearls of Wisdom,* vol. 36, no. 21, May 23, 1993.

11. Ibid.
12. Ibid.
13. Peace and Aloha, June 12, 1976.
14. Peace, March 26, 1978.
15. Luke 11:14, 24–26.
16. Peace and Aloha, June 10, 1984, *Pearls of Wisdom*, vol. 32, no. 14, April 2, 1989.
17. Elohim of Peace, July 4, 1992, "The Crown Jewel of Peace," in *Pearls of Wisdom*, vol. 35, no. 43, October 14, 1992.
18. Peace and Aloha, June 10, 1984.
19. Peace and Aloha, June 12, 1976.
20. Ibid.
21. Peace and Aloha, June 10, 1984.
22. Ibid.
23. Peace and Aloha, April 8, 1993.
24. Ibid.
25. Ibid.
26. Ibid.
27. Ibid.
28. Saint Germain's Heart Meditations I and II, delivered by the messenger at Saint Germain's request, are for the clearing, strengthening and initiation of the heart chakra and the balancing of the threefold flame. They include devotional prayers, decrees, mantras, hymns, meditations and visualizations as well as instruction and invocations by the messenger and the opportunity for participants to offer personal prayers. For ordering information, contact Summit University Press.
29. Peace and Aloha, April 8, 1993.
30. Peace, March 26, 1978.
31. Peace, April 1, 1988, "The Meaning of Peace," in *Pearls of Wisdom*, vol. 31, no. 45, July 27, 1988.
32. Peace, August 11, 1991.
33. Ibid.
34. Ibid.
35. Ibid.
36. Peace, January 2, 1972, "An Experience in the Pavilion of Peace," excerpted in "The Radiant Word," in *Pearls of Wisdom*, vol. 15, no. 18, April 30, 1972.
37. Peace and Aloha, April 8, 1993.
38. Matt. 10:34.

Fallen Angels and the Origins of Evil

Saint Germain's Prophecy for the New Millennium

The Lost Years of Jesus

The Lost Teachings of Jesus (4 vols.)

Inner Perspectives

Keys to the Kingdom

The Human Aura

Saint Germain On Alchemy

The Science of the Spoken Word

Kabbalah: Key to Your Inner Power

Reincarnation: The Missing Link in Christianity

Quietly Comes the Buddha

Lords of the Seven Rays

Prayer and Meditation

The Chela and the Path

Mysteries of the Holy Grail

Dossier on the Ascension

The Path to Your Ascension

Understanding Yourself

Secrets of Prosperity

The Answer You're Looking for Is Inside of You

The Opening of the Temple Doors

Nurturing Your Baby's Soul

Sacred Psychology of Love

Sacred Psychology of Change

Dreams: Exploring the Secrets of Your Soul

Emotions: Transforming Anger, Fear and Pain

Soul Reflections: Many Lives, Many Journeys

A Spiritual Approach to Parenting

FOR MORE INFORMATION

Summit University Press books are available at fine bookstores worldwide and at your favorite on-line bookseller. For a free catalog of our books and products or to learn more about the spiritual techniques featured in this book, please contact:

Summit University Press
PO Box 5000
Gardiner, MT 59030-5000 USA
Telephone: 1-800-245-5445 or 406-848-9500
Fax: 1-800-221-8307 or 406-848-9555
www.summituniversitypress.com
info@summituniversitypress.com

Mark L. Prophet and Elizabeth Clare Prophet are pioneers of modern spirituality and internationally renowned authors. Among their best-selling titles are *The Lost Years of Jesus, The Lost Teachings of Jesus, The Human Aura, Saint Germain On Alchemy, Fallen Angels and the Origins of Evil* and the Pocket Guides to Practical Spirituality series, which includes *How to Work with Angels, Your Seven Energy Centers* and *Soul Mates and Twin Flames*. Their books are now translated into more than twenty languages and are available in more than thirty countries.